Innovative Robotics with ROS2 and Python

Advanced Concepts for Building Intelligent, Interactive, and Multi-Robot Systems

Thompson Carter

Rafael Sanders

Miguel Farmer

Copyright © 2025

Contents

[5]

[11]

How to Scan a Barcode to Get a Repository

1. **Install a QR/Barcode Scanner** – Ensure you have a barcode or **QR** code scanner app installed on your smartphone or use a built-in scanner in **GitHub, GitLab, or Bitbucket.**

2. **Open the Scanner** – Launch the scanner app and grant necessary camera permissions.

3. **Scan the Barcode** – Align the barcode within the scanning frame. The scanner will automatically detect and process it.

4. **Follow the Link** – The scanned result will display a **URL to the repository.** Tap the link to open it in your web browser or Git client.

5. **Clone the Repository** – Use **Git clone** with the provided URL to download the repository to your local machine.

Chapter 1: Introduction

Welcome to the exciting realm of robotics! In this opening chapter, we'll embark on a journey designed to introduce you to the world of robotics—its basic principles, its incredible evolution over time, and the powerful impact it has on industries and everyday life. Whether you're completely new to robotics or have dabbled in technology before, this chapter is crafted to be your friendly guide, filled with clear explanations, engaging analogies, and practical, step-by-step insights. Let's dive in and explore how robotics can transform your future, one step at a time.

---

1. Understanding Robotics: A Beginner's Perspective

Imagine a world where machines not only perform repetitive tasks but also learn, adapt, and even interact with their human counterparts. This is the promise of robotics—a field that fuses mechanical engineering, electronics, and computer science to create devices capable of performing tasks autonomously or semi-autonomously.

What Exactly Is a Robot?

In simple terms, a **robot** is a machine that can execute a series of actions automatically. These actions can range from simple, repetitive tasks to complex operations that require decision-making and interaction. Think of a robot as your digital helper: just like a personal assistant, it carries out commands, processes information, and can work tirelessly without the need for breaks.

Key Components of a Robot

To demystify the concept further, let's break down the main components that make up a robot:

1. **Sensors:**

   - **Purpose:** To detect changes in the environment.

   - **Examples:** Cameras, LIDAR, infrared sensors.

   - **Analogy:** Think of sensors as a robot's "eyes" and "ears" that help it understand what's happening around it.

2. **Actuators:**

   - **Purpose:** To perform physical actions.

   - **Examples:** Motors, servos, hydraulic systems.

   - **Analogy:** If sensors are the senses, actuators are the muscles that enable movement.

3. **Control Unit (Brain):**

   - **Purpose:** To process data from sensors and make decisions.

   - **Examples:** Microcontrollers, CPUs running complex software.

- ○ **Analogy:** The control unit is like a human brain, orchestrating responses based on sensory input.

4. **Power Supply:**

   - ○ **Purpose:** To provide energy for all the robot's functions.

   - ○ **Examples:** Batteries, solar panels, power cables.

   - ○ **Analogy:** Just as food fuels our bodies, the power supply energizes the robot.

5. **Communication Interfaces:**

   - ○ **Purpose:** To exchange information with other systems or humans.

   - ○ **Examples:** Wi-Fi, Bluetooth, Ethernet.

   - ○ **Analogy:** Consider these the robot's "mouth" and "ears" when it needs to talk or listen.

The Anatomy of a Robot

Below is a simplified diagram that illustrates the fundamental components of a typical robot:

```
+-------------------------+
|       Sensors           |
|   (Eyes, Ears, etc.)|
+-------------------------+
             |
             v
+-------------------------+
|     Control Unit        |
|      (The Brain)        |
+-------------------------+
             |
+-------------------------+
|                         |
v                         v
+------------------+   +------------------+
| Actuators |      |   | Power    |
| (Muscles) |      |   | Supply   |
+------------------+   +------------------+
             |
             v
+-------------------------+
|   Communication         |
|   Interfaces            |
+-------------------------+
```

This diagram provides a clear visual guide to understanding how sensors, control units, actuators, power supplies, and communication interfaces interact to form a functional robot.

Why Start Your Robotics Journey?

Have you ever wondered why robotics is so captivating? Let's explore a few reasons:

- **Curiosity and Creativity:**
  Robotics is a perfect playground for creative minds. Imagine building a machine that can solve real-world problems—whether it's navigating obstacles in a warehouse or assisting with complex surgical procedures.

- **Real-World Impact:**
  From manufacturing to healthcare, robotics is reshaping industries. By understanding robotics, you're not just learning about technology—you're preparing to be part of a movement that can change lives.

- **Problem-Solving Skills:**
  Working with robotics helps you develop a systematic approach to solving problems. Each challenge, from debugging code to integrating a new sensor, hones your analytical and creative thinking.

- **Future-Proofing Your Career:**
  As technology continues to evolve, robotics skills are increasingly in demand. Whether you aspire to join a

tech giant or launch your own startup, mastering robotics opens up countless opportunities.

Step-by-Step: How to Think About Robotics

Let's break down your approach to learning robotics into actionable steps:

1. **Start with the Basics:**

   o **Action:** Understand the core components of a robot and basic programming concepts.

   o **Tip:** Don't be overwhelmed by technical jargon; focus on grasping fundamental ideas first.

2. **Explore Hands-On Projects:**

   o **Action:** Begin with simple projects like building a basic sensor circuit or programming a microcontroller.

   o **Tip:** Use online tutorials and community forums for guidance.

3. **Join a Community:**

   o **Action:** Connect with fellow enthusiasts through clubs, online forums, or local workshops.

   o **Tip:** Collaboration and discussion are key to overcoming challenges.

4. **Experiment and Iterate:**

- o **Action:** Embrace trial and error. Build, test, and refine your projects.

- o **Tip:** Document your progress and learn from each experiment.

5. **Expand Your Knowledge:**

- o **Action:** Once comfortable with basics, delve into advanced topics like machine learning and robotic simulation.

- o **Tip:** Keep challenging yourself with progressively complex projects.

Engaging Question:

Have you ever built something from scratch and felt the thrill of watching it come to life? That's the magic of robotics—each project is a new adventure waiting to unfold!

---

2. The Evolution of Robotics: From Concept to Reality

Robotics has a rich history filled with innovation, challenges, and breakthroughs. Understanding its evolution helps you appreciate not only where we are today but also where we're headed tomorrow.

A Brief History: Milestones in Robotics

The journey of robotics is like an epic story with many chapters. Here are some key milestones:

1. **Early Automatons:**

   - **What They Were:** Simple mechanical devices designed to mimic human or animal behavior.

   - **Historical Context:** Ancient civilizations crafted ingenious devices powered by water or air.

   - **Impact:** Laid the groundwork for the concept of machines that can perform tasks automatically.

2. **Industrial Revolution:**

   - **What Happened:** The rise of mechanization and assembly lines.

   - **Historical Context:** Factories began incorporating automated machinery to boost production.

   - **Impact:** Introduced the idea of robots in manufacturing, paving the way for modern industrial robots.

3. **The Advent of Computers:**

   - **What Changed:** The integration of digital technology allowed for precise control and programmability.

   - **Historical Context:** The mid-20th century saw the birth of computer-controlled machinery.

- o **Impact:** Enabled the development of robots that could perform complex tasks with high accuracy.

4. **Modern Robotics:**

   - o **What's New:** The fusion of artificial intelligence (AI), advanced sensors, and agile control systems.

   - o **Historical Context:** Recent decades have witnessed rapid advancements in machine learning and connectivity.

   - o **Impact:** Today's robots can navigate dynamic environments, learn from experiences, and interact intelligently with humans.

Robotics Evolution Timeline

Below is a timeline diagram that visually summarizes the key milestones in the evolution of robotics:

```
[ Ancient Automatons ]
        |
        v
[ Industrial Revolution ]
        |
        v
[ Computer-Controlled Robotics ]
        |
        v
[ Modern Robotics (AI & Connectivity) ]
```

This simple timeline illustrates the progression from early mechanical devices to the sophisticated, intelligent robots of today. Each stage represents a leap in innovation and capability.

The Driving Forces Behind Robotic Evolution

Robotic evolution has been fueled by several factors that continue to shape its development:

- **Technological Advancements:**

  - **Microprocessors and Sensors:** Innovations in electronics have allowed robots to become more compact, efficient, and capable.

  - **Software Development:** Advances in programming and algorithms have enabled robots to process data faster and make smarter decisions.

- **Economic and Industrial Demands:**

  - **Efficiency:** Industries have long sought to automate repetitive tasks, reducing human error and increasing productivity.

  - **Safety:** Robots can operate in hazardous environments where human presence might be risky, such as in nuclear plants or deep-sea explorations.

- **Scientific Curiosity:**

- ○ **Research and Exploration:** Scientists and engineers are driven by a desire to push boundaries, leading to groundbreaking research in robotics.

- ○ **Interdisciplinary Collaboration:** The integration of fields like biology, physics, and computer science has led to innovative designs and applications.

Engaging Your Imagination

Have you ever wondered how far robotics has come? Picture an ancient automaton, a cleverly engineered clockwork figure that moves with surprising grace. Fast forward to today, and imagine robots that can perform delicate surgeries, navigate Mars, or assist in disaster relief. Each leap in robotics has been driven by human ingenuity and the desire to improve our world.

Step-by-Step: Reflecting on the Past to Build the Future

Let's consider a step-by-step approach to understanding how the past influences modern robotics:

1. **Explore Historical Examples:**

   - ○ **Action:** Read about early automatons and industrial robots.

   - ○ **Tip:** Look for documentaries or books that explain these concepts in simple terms.

2. **Identify Key Innovations:**

  - o **Action:** Make a list of technological breakthroughs that revolutionized robotics (e.g., microprocessors, AI).

  - o **Tip:** Use online resources and timelines to gather your information.

3. **Analyze Their Impact:**

  - o **Action:** Reflect on how each innovation improved robot capabilities.

  - o **Tip:** Write down how these changes affect industries today.

4. **Visualize the Progression:**

  - o **Action:** Create your own timeline of robotic evolution.

  - o **Tip:** Use simple drawing tools or even pen and paper to map out the evolution.

5. **Envision the Future:**

  - o **Action:** Consider how emerging technologies might further change robotics.

  - o **Tip:** Join online forums or attend tech meetups to discuss future trends.

Rhetorical Question:
Isn't it fascinating to think that the simple machines of the past have evolved into the intelligent systems we see today?

The journey of robotics is not just about technology—it's a story of human innovation and resilience.

---

3. Why Robotics Matters: Transforming Industries and Lives

In a world that's constantly evolving, robotics stands out as one of the most transformative technologies of our time. Its influence reaches far beyond the realm of factories and laboratories—it's changing the way we live, work, and interact with our surroundings.

Robotics in Everyday Life

Imagine waking up in the morning and having your coffee brewed automatically, your home adjusted to the perfect temperature, and your schedule organized by an intelligent assistant. These are not scenes from a futuristic movie—they're real-world applications of robotics that are becoming increasingly common in our daily lives.

Real-World Applications

- **Manufacturing:**
  - **What Happens:** Robots work alongside humans on assembly lines to increase precision and speed.
  - **Impact:** Improved product quality and reduced production costs.

- **Healthcare:**

  - **What Happens:** Robots assist in surgeries, deliver medications, and even help patients with rehabilitation.

  - **Impact:** Enhanced patient care, reduced recovery times, and improved surgical outcomes.

- **Agriculture:**

  - **What Happens:** Automated systems monitor crop health, manage irrigation, and even harvest produce.

  - **Impact:** Increased crop yields, reduced labor costs, and more sustainable farming practices.

- **Logistics and Warehousing:**

  - **What Happens:** Robots navigate warehouses to move goods efficiently, from inventory management to order fulfillment.

  - **Impact:** Faster delivery times and streamlined operations.

Industries Transformed by Robotics

Below is a diagram that maps out how robotics is impacting different industries:

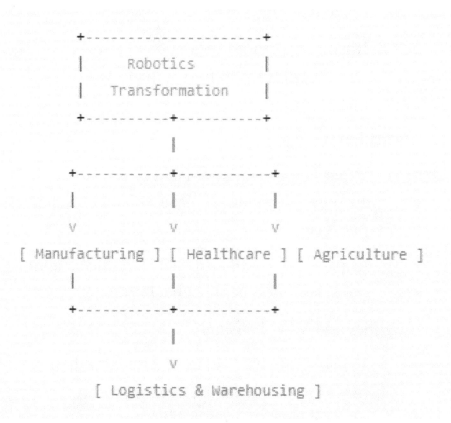

This diagram visually demonstrates the interconnected impact of robotics on various sectors. Each industry benefits uniquely, contributing to a more efficient and innovative future.

How Robotics Is Changing Lives

Robotics is not only transforming industries—it's also revolutionizing the way people live. Consider these personal and societal benefits:

- **Enhanced Safety:**
  Robots can take on dangerous tasks in environments where human safety would be at risk, such as in hazardous material handling or disaster response.

- **Increased Efficiency:**
  Automation reduces repetitive manual labor, allowing people to focus on more creative and strategic endeavors.

- **Improved Accessibility:**
  Assistive robots are empowering individuals with disabilities, offering support for daily tasks and increasing independence.

- **Innovation in Services:**
  From smart homes to autonomous vehicles, robotics is redefining convenience and connectivity.

Step-by-Step: Recognizing the Impact of Robotics

Let's walk through a structured approach to understanding how robotics is making a difference:

1. **Identify Daily Challenges:**
   - o **Action:** List tasks in your daily routine that could be automated (e.g., cleaning, scheduling, transportation).
   - o **Tip:** Reflect on areas where you feel overwhelmed or limited by manual processes.

2. **Explore Current Solutions:**

   o **Action:** Research existing robotic solutions addressing these challenges.

   o **Tip:** Watch videos or read case studies on robots in action.

3. **Evaluate the Benefits:**

   o **Action:** Note down the advantages of using robotic solutions, such as time savings, increased safety, or enhanced accuracy.

   o **Tip:** Compare these benefits against traditional methods.

4. **Consider Future Innovations:**

   o **Action:** Imagine how robotics could further enhance these areas.

   o **Tip:** Engage in discussions or brainstorming sessions with friends or online communities.

5. **Apply the Insights:**

   o **Action:** Think about how you might incorporate robotic solutions into your work or personal projects.

   o **Tip:** Start small and build your understanding progressively.

Rhetorical Question:
Have you ever experienced the relief of having a task

automated? Robotics empowers us to reclaim time and energy, allowing us to focus on what truly matters.

---

4. Unleashing the Power of ROS2 and Python: The Future is Now

As you venture further into robotics, you'll soon discover that two powerful tools are revolutionizing the way robots are built and programmed: **ROS2** (Robot Operating System 2) and **Python**. Together, they offer a flexible, scalable, and intuitive framework for developing sophisticated robotic applications.

Why ROS2?

ROS2 is an open-source framework designed specifically for robotics. It provides a standardized set of tools, libraries, and conventions that make it easier for developers to build, test, and deploy robotic systems.

Key Benefits of ROS2

- **Modularity:**
  ROS2 allows you to break down complex robotic systems into smaller, manageable modules known as "nodes." Each node handles a specific task, making it easier to troubleshoot and upgrade individual components.

- **Real-Time Performance:**
  With enhanced capabilities for real-time processing, ROS2 ensures that your robot can react quickly to changes in its environment—a critical requirement for applications such as autonomous vehicles or robotic surgery.

- **Scalability:**
  Whether you're programming a single robot or a fleet of collaborative machines, ROS2 scales seamlessly to meet your needs.

- **Community Support:**
  An active community of developers contributes to ROS2, ensuring a rich ecosystem of packages, tutorials, and troubleshooting guides.

The ROS2 Ecosystem

Below is a diagram that shows how ROS2 organizes a robotic system into interconnected nodes and communication channels:

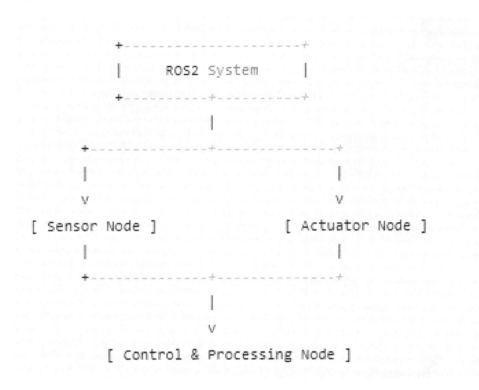

This diagram illustrates the modular design of ROS2. Sensors, actuators, and control nodes communicate seamlessly, ensuring that the entire system functions in harmony.

The Role of Python in Robotics

Python is celebrated for its readability, simplicity, and powerful libraries. In robotics, Python serves as an excellent tool for scripting and rapid prototyping.

Why Choose Python?

- **Ease of Learning:**
Python's clear syntax and straightforward semantics make it accessible even for those who are new to programming.

- **Versatile Libraries:**
With libraries like NumPy for numerical computations, OpenCV for computer vision, and TensorFlow for machine learning, Python equips you with a wide array of tools to enhance your robotic projects.

- **Community and Resources:**
A vibrant community ensures that help is always available. Whether you're stuck on a bug or searching for inspiration, countless tutorials and forums are at your disposal.

- **Integration with ROS2:**
ROS2's Python client library, rclpy, allows you to write ROS2 nodes in Python, combining the best of both worlds: the robust, real-time capabilities of ROS2 and the rapid development prowess of Python.

How ROS2 and Python Work Together

Below is a simplified flowchart that depicts the interaction between ROS2 and Python in a robotic system:

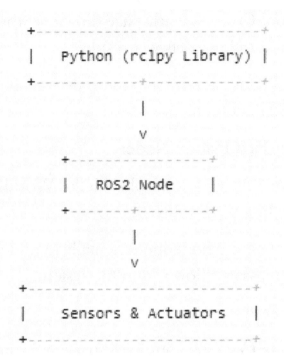

This flowchart shows how Python, through the rclpy library, enables you to create ROS2 nodes that interact directly with the hardware components of your robot.

Step-by-Step: Integrating ROS2 and Python

Let's break down the process of integrating these powerful tools into your robotics projects:

1. **Install ROS2 and Python:**

   o **Action:** Follow detailed installation guides to set up ROS2 (e.g., ROS2 Humble) and ensure Python 3.x is installed.

- o **Tip:** Use virtual environments to manage dependencies effectively.

2. **Set Up a ROS2 Workspace:**

   - o **Action:** Create a workspace directory where your ROS2 projects will reside.

   - o **Tip:** Follow step-by-step tutorials available in the ROS2 documentation.

3. **Write Your First Python Node:**

   - o **Action:** Develop a simple "Hello, World!" node in Python using rclpy.

   - o **Tip:** Test the node incrementally to understand how messages flow within the system.

4. **Build and Test:**

   - o **Action:** Compile your workspace and run the node to see it in action.

   - o **Tip:** Use ROS2's built-in debugging tools to troubleshoot any issues.

5. **Expand Gradually:**

   - o **Action:** Once comfortable with basic nodes, experiment with integrating sensor data and actuator commands.

   - o **Tip:** Refer to community projects and open-source repositories for inspiration and best practices.

Rhetorical Question:

Isn't it empowering to know that you can combine the simplicity of Python with the robust features of ROS2 to build intelligent robots? This synergy opens up endless possibilities for innovation.

---

5. Charting Your Path: A Step-by-Step Guide to Start Your Robotics Journey

Now that you understand what robotics is, its evolution, and the power behind tools like ROS2 and Python, it's time to plan your journey forward. Whether you're aiming to build your first robot or develop advanced robotic systems, having a clear roadmap is essential.

Defining Your Goals

Before you start, ask yourself: What do you want to achieve with robotics? Your goals will shape your learning path and projects. Here are some common aspirations:

- **Learning the Basics:**
  If you're new to robotics, your first goal might be to understand the core principles and build simple projects.

- **Creating Functional Prototypes:**
  For those with some experience, the goal might be to develop prototypes that perform specific tasks—like a mobile robot that navigates a room.

- **Solving Real-World Problems:**
  More advanced enthusiasts might aim to address complex challenges in industries such as healthcare, manufacturing, or logistics.

- **Innovating and Experimenting:**
  Some may simply be driven by the joy of tinkering and innovation, pushing the boundaries of what robots can do.

Step-by-Step: Planning Your Robotics Journey

Let's break down a detailed, actionable plan to kick-start your robotics adventure:

1. **Set Clear Objectives:**

   - **Action:** Write down what you hope to achieve.
   - **Example:** "I want to build a robot that can navigate my home autonomously."
   - **Tip:** Be specific and realistic with your goals.

2. **Gather Resources:**

   - **Action:** Identify the tools, tutorials, and communities that will support your learning.
   - **Resources May Include:**
     - Online courses (e.g., Coursera, Udemy)

- Forums and discussion groups (e.g., ROS Discourse, Reddit's robotics community)

- Books and documentation (e.g., official ROS2 tutorials)

  o **Tip:** Bookmark helpful websites and maintain a resource list.

3. **Plan Your Projects:**

   o **Action:** Break down your goal into smaller, manageable projects.

   o **Example Projects:**

     - Create a basic sensor integration project.

     - Develop a simple ROS2 node in Python.

     - Simulate a mobile robot in a virtual environment.

   o **Tip:** Use a project management tool or a simple checklist to keep track of your progress.

4. **Allocate Time for Learning and Experimentation:**

   o **Action:** Designate regular time slots in your schedule for working on robotics.

   o **Tip:** Consistency is key—small, regular sessions often lead to steady progress.

5. **Engage with the Community:**

- o **Action:** Attend workshops, join online forums, and collaborate on projects.

- o **Tip:** Sharing your experiences and challenges with others can lead to valuable insights and support.

6. **Document Your Journey:**

- o **Action:** Keep a journal or blog of your projects, challenges, and breakthroughs.

- o **Tip:** Documentation not only helps you reflect on your progress but can also assist others who are on a similar path.

Embracing Challenges and Celebrating Wins

Robotics is as much about learning from failures as it is about celebrating successes. Every challenge you face is an opportunity to improve and innovate.

- **Common Challenges:**
  - o Debugging code and hardware issues.
  - o Integrating multiple components seamlessly.
  - o Balancing theory with practical application.

- **How to Overcome Them:**
  - o **Research:** Look up similar problems online or ask in forums.

- o **Experiment:** Try different approaches until you find a solution.

- o **Collaborate:** Don't hesitate to seek help from more experienced enthusiasts.

Engaging Thought:
Remember, every expert was once a beginner. The obstacles you encounter are stepping stones toward mastery.

Actionable Project: Your First Robotics Blueprint

Let's conclude this chapter with a hands-on mini-project to kickstart your robotics journey:

Project Title: *"Home Navigator: A Simple Autonomous Robot"*

Objective:
Build a simple robot that can navigate a predefined path in your home using basic sensors and a Python-controlled ROS2 node.

Step-by-Step Instructions:

1. **Define the Requirements:**
   - o **List the Components:**
     - Basic chassis and wheels
     - Ultrasonic sensor for obstacle detection
     - Microcontroller or single-board computer

- Power supply (batteries)

  o **Set the Goal:**

    - The robot should move forward and stop or change direction when an obstacle is detected.

2. **Design the Layout:**

   o **Create a Rough Sketch:**

     - Draw a simple layout of the robot, indicating sensor positions and wiring.

   o **Robot Layout Sketch**

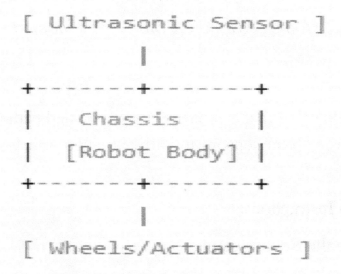

```
[ Ultrasonic Sensor ]
         |
+--------+--------+
|     Chassis     |
|   [Robot Body]  |
+--------+--------+
         |
[ Wheels/Actuators ]
```

This sketch shows a basic design where the sensor is positioned at the front, providing a clear line of sight for obstacle detection.

3. **Develop the Software:**

- o **Set Up Your Environment:**
  - Install ROS2 and Python on your computer.
  - Create a new ROS2 workspace.
- o **Write a Basic Python Node:**
  - Create a node that reads sensor data and sends movement commands.
  - Use clear, step-by-step comments in your code.

4. **Test and Iterate:**
   - o **Run the Node in Simulation:**
     - Use a simulation tool (like Gazebo) to test your robot's behavior before hardware implementation.
   - o **Refine the Code:**
     - Adjust sensor thresholds and movement parameters based on testing feedback.

5. **Document Your Process:**
   - o **Keep a Log:**
     - Record what worked, what didn't, and how you resolved issues.
   - o **Share Your Experience:**

- Consider posting your progress on a robotics forum or blog for additional insights.

Encouraging Note:
Every line of code you write and every prototype you build is a step forward in your robotics journey. Embrace the challenges, learn from each mistake, and celebrate every small success.

Final Thoughts

Your journey into robotics is just beginning, and the possibilities are as limitless as your imagination. From understanding the basics to exploring cutting-edge tools like ROS2 and Python, each step you take is a leap toward a future where robots not only assist but also inspire. Remember, robotics is not about being perfect—it's about progress, creativity, and a relentless drive to explore new horizons.

Reflective Question:
What problem in your daily life or work would you like to solve with robotics? Let that question guide your projects and fuel your passion.

As you continue this journey, keep this chapter as a reminder of where you started and the endless potential that lies ahead. The world of robotics awaits your unique ideas and innovations. Happy building, and welcome to the future of technology!

Chapter 2: Setting Up Your Development Environment

Welcome to one of the most exciting parts of your robotics journey—getting your development environment ready to build, test, and innovate with ROS2 and Python! Think of this as preparing your very own workshop, where every tool is in its place and every system is ready to help you transform ideas into reality. In this chapter, we'll walk through the process step by step, ensuring that everything is crystal clear, jargon-free, and accessible—no matter your experience level.

Throughout this chapter, you'll find diagrams that visually simplify complex workflows, practical checklists to keep you on track, and engaging analogies that connect technical concepts to everyday experiences. So, let's roll up our sleeves and dive into the process of setting up your development environment.

---

1. Introduction: Why a Solid Development Environment Matters

Before we jump into the nuts and bolts of installation and configuration, let's pause for a moment. Have you ever tried building a piece of furniture without the proper tools? It might be possible, but it's certainly not efficient, and you may end up with a wobbly table. Similarly, in robotics, a well-organized development environment is the foundation upon which reliable, efficient, and innovative projects are built.

The Importance of a Clean Setup

A clean development environment:

- **Reduces Errors:** By isolating your tools and dependencies, you minimize conflicts that might cause confusing errors.

- **Boosts Productivity:** When everything is set up correctly, you spend less time troubleshooting and more time creating.

- **Enhances Learning:** A properly configured workspace makes it easier to follow tutorials, replicate experiments, and build upon your projects.

What Will You Learn in This Chapter?

In this chapter, you will:

1. **Install Your Operating System Essentials:** Understand the basics of what you need to run ROS2 and Python.

2. **Set Up ROS2:** Get the latest version of ROS2 installed, explained in clear, simple language.

3. **Install Python and Create a Virtual Environment:**
   Learn why Python is the perfect companion for
   robotics and how to manage it effectively.

4. **Integrate ROS2 with Python:** Discover how these two
   tools work together seamlessly.

5. **Configure Your Workspace:** Set up your project
   folders and tools for an organized coding experience.

6. **Test and Troubleshoot:** Ensure everything is working
   with practical, step-by-step testing.

The Development Environment Overview

Below is a simple diagram that gives you a bird's-eye view of the development environment setup:

```
+-------------------------------+
|    Operating System           |
| (Linux/Windows/macOS)         |
+--------------+----------------+
               |
               v
+-------------------------------+
|    ROS2 Installation          |
| (Middleware for Robotics)     |
+--------------+----------------+
               |
               v
+-------------------------------+
| Python & Virtual Environment|
| (Programming & Dependency     |
|    Management)                |
+--------------+----------------+
               |
               v
+-------------------------------+
|    Workspace Setup            |
| (Code, Projects, Tools)       |
+-------------------------------+
```

This diagram offers a clear snapshot of how each component of your development environment interconnects. Think of it as your roadmap to building a robust platform for your robotics projects.

---

2. Installing Your Operating System and Essential Software

Before installing ROS2 or Python, you need a solid foundation: your operating system and essential software tools. For robotics development, many enthusiasts prefer Linux due to its compatibility and support with ROS2, though Windows and macOS are also viable options. Let's break this down into simple steps.

Choosing the Right Operating System

Why Linux?
Linux is renowned for its stability, security, and open-source nature. It's widely used in robotics because:

- **Compatibility:** Many ROS2 packages and tools are developed for Linux.

- **Community Support:** A vast community of developers provides support and tutorials.

- **Customization:** Linux is highly customizable, allowing you to tailor your environment.

But what if you prefer Windows or macOS?
Don't worry—ROS2 and Python work on these systems as

well. Just be sure to check the installation guides for any platform-specific instructions.

Step-by-Step: Installing Essential Software

1. **Update Your Operating System:**

   o **Action:** Ensure your OS is updated with the latest security patches and system updates.

   o **Tip:** On Linux, you might run a command like sudo apt update && sudo apt upgrade to keep your system current.

2. **Install a Terminal Emulator:**

   o **Action:** If your OS doesn't come with a robust terminal, install one (e.g., GNOME Terminal for Linux, Windows Terminal for Windows, or iTerm2 for macOS).

   o **Tip:** A good terminal makes navigating your system and running commands much more enjoyable.

3. **Install a Code Editor or IDE:**

   o **Action:** Choose an editor that suits your needs— VSCode, PyCharm, or even Sublime Text.

   o **Tip:** Visual Studio Code is a popular choice due to its extensive plugin ecosystem and user-friendly interface.

4. **Install Version Control Software:**

- o **Action:** Download and install Git. It's essential for managing your code and collaborating with others.

- o **Tip:** Familiarize yourself with basic Git commands like clone, commit, and push.

5. **Set Up Basic Utilities:**

- o **Action:** Install utilities such as curl, wget, and build-essential (on Linux) to handle downloads and software compilation.

- o **Tip:** These tools are often used in installation scripts and troubleshooting, so having them ready can save you time later.

Essential Software Installation Flow

Below is a simple diagram that illustrates the steps to install essential software:

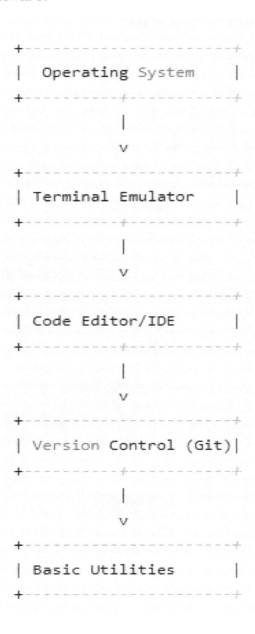

This flowchart visually represents the sequence of software installations required to lay the groundwork for your development environment.

Why These Tools Matter

- **Terminal Emulator:** Your command line interface is like the control panel for your workshop. It's where you run commands, execute scripts, and interact directly with your system.

- **Code Editor/IDE:** Think of this as your drafting table. It's where you write and organize your code, debug your projects, and manage files.

- **Git:** Version control is essential, much like saving multiple drafts of a document. Git ensures you can track changes, collaborate effectively, and revert to previous versions if something goes wrong.

- **Basic Utilities:** These are your general-purpose tools, the equivalent of screwdrivers and pliers in a physical workshop. They help you install, update, and troubleshoot your software.

By taking these steps, you ensure that your operating system is ready to support the advanced tools you'll install next.

3. Installing ROS2: Your Middleware for Robotics

Now that your operating system and essential software are ready, it's time to install ROS2 (Robot Operating System 2). ROS2 is the heart of many robotics projects, providing a modular and scalable framework for communication between software components.

What is ROS2 and Why Use It?

ROS2 in Simple Terms:
ROS2 is like the nervous system of a robot. It allows different parts of the robot to talk to each other, coordinate tasks, and react to real-world events. With ROS2, you can build systems that are modular, meaning you can develop and test individual parts without affecting the whole system.

Benefits of ROS2:

- **Modularity:** Breaks your robot's functions into manageable pieces called nodes.

- **Real-Time Capabilities:** Essential for applications that need quick responses.

- **Cross-Platform Support:** Works on Linux, Windows, and macOS.

- **Community and Resources:** A thriving community means you can always find help and tutorials.

Step-by-Step: Installing ROS2

1. **Check Your Operating System Compatibility:**

   - o **Action:** Verify that your OS version is supported by the ROS2 distribution you plan to install (e.g., ROS2 Humble, Foxy).

   - o **Tip:** Visit the official ROS2 website for a list of supported systems and installation instructions.

2. **Set Up Your Sources:**

   - o **Action:** Add the ROS2 repository to your system's package manager. For Ubuntu, this often involves adding a new repository via the terminal.

   - o **Tip:** Follow the instructions provided on the ROS2 website to ensure you're adding the correct keys and sources.

3. **Install ROS2 Packages:**

   - o **Action:** Use your package manager (e.g., apt on Ubuntu) to install ROS2 packages.

   - o **Command Example (Ubuntu):**

```bash


sudo apt update
sudo apt install ros-humble-desktop
```

- o **Tip:** The ros-humble-desktop package is a common choice that includes many useful tools for development.

4. **Initialize ROS2 Environment Variables:**

- o **Action:** Source the ROS2 setup file to ensure your environment variables are set correctly.

- o **Command Example:**

```bash
```

```bash
source /opt/ros/humble/setup.bash
```

- o **Tip:** To automate this, add the command to your shell's startup file (e.g., .bashrc).

5. **Verify the Installation:**

- o **Action:** Run a simple ROS2 command or launch a demo to confirm that ROS2 is installed correctly.

- o **Tip:** Try running ros2 run demo_nodes_cpp talker and ros2 run demo_nodes_cpp listener in separate terminals to see if the nodes communicate.

Common Pitfalls and How to Avoid Them

- **Repository Issues:**

  - o *Problem:* Incorrect repository or missing keys.

- o *Solution:* Double-check the ROS2 website for the correct repository URLs and instructions.

- **Environment Variables Not Set:**

  - o *Problem:* ROS2 commands not recognized.

  - o *Solution:* Ensure you source the setup file after installation or add it to your startup script.

- **Package Dependencies:**

  - o *Problem:* Missing dependencies leading to installation errors.

  - o *Solution:* Use the package manager to install missing dependencies, and refer to error messages for guidance.

By following these steps, you'll have ROS2 up and running, ready to serve as the backbone of your robotics projects.

---

4. Installing Python and Creating a Virtual Environment

With ROS2 installed, the next step is to set up Python. Python is the programming language that will help you script your robots, process data, and tie everything together. To keep your project organized and avoid conflicts between different software packages, creating a virtual environment is essential.

Why Python?

Python's Role in Robotics:

Python is known for its simplicity, readability, and versatility. It's like the Swiss Army knife of programming languages—ready to tackle a wide range of tasks with minimal fuss. In robotics, Python enables rapid prototyping, easy integration with ROS2 through the rclpy library, and access to a vast ecosystem of libraries for tasks like data processing and machine learning.

Benefits of Using Python:

- **User-Friendly:** Its clear syntax makes it easy to learn and use.

- **Powerful Libraries:** Libraries like NumPy, OpenCV, and TensorFlow extend Python's functionality.

- **Wide Adoption:** A large community means abundant resources and support.

Step-by-Step: Installing Python

1. **Check Your Python Version:**

   - **Action:** Open your terminal and type python3 --version to see which version is installed.

   - **Tip:** ROS2 typically works well with Python 3. Ensure you have Python 3.x installed.

2. **Download Python (if needed):**

- o **Action:** If Python isn't installed, visit python.org to download the latest version.

- o **Tip:** Follow the installation instructions for your operating system.

3. **Install Python via Package Manager:**

- o **Action:** On Linux, you might run:

bash

```
sudo apt install python3 python3-pip
```

- o **Tip:** Pip, the Python package installer, will be invaluable for managing additional libraries.

Creating a Virtual Environment

A virtual environment is like a sandbox where you can safely install and manage libraries without affecting the global system. This isolation prevents conflicts and ensures that your projects remain self-contained.

1. **Install the Virtual Environment Package:**

- o **Action:** Run:

bash

```
sudo apt install python3-venv
```

- o **Tip:** This package provides the tools necessary to create isolated environments.

2. **Create a New Virtual Environment:**

- o **Action:** Navigate to your project directory and create a new virtual environment:

bash

```
python3 -m venv my_robot_env
```

- o **Tip:** Replace my_robot_env with a name that reflects your project.

3. **Activate the Virtual Environment:**

- o **Action:** Activate the environment with:

bash

```
source my_robot_env/bin/activate
```

- o **Tip:** Once activated, your terminal prompt will change to indicate that you're working inside the virtual environment.

4. **Install Essential Python Libraries:**

- o **Action:** Within your virtual environment, install libraries such as rclpy, numpy, and others you may need:

bash

```
pip install rclpy numpy
```

- o **Tip:** Maintain a requirements.txt file for easy replication of your environment later.

The Benefits of a Virtual Environment

- **Isolation:** Keeps your project's dependencies separate from system-wide installations.

- **Reproducibility:** Makes it easier to share your project with others or move it to another machine.

- **Flexibility:** Allows you to experiment with different library versions without impacting your main system.

By following these steps, you're ensuring that your Python environment is robust, manageable, and ready to support your robotics projects.

---

5. Integrating ROS2 with Python

With both ROS2 and Python set up, it's time to bring them together. Integrating ROS2 with Python allows you to harness the power of ROS2's middleware using Python's simplicity and flexibility. This integration is made possible by the rclpy library, which acts as a bridge between the two.

What is rclpy?

Understanding rclpy:
rclpy is the Python client library for ROS2. It enables you to write ROS2 nodes in Python, allowing you to control sensors, actuators, and process data—all with a few lines of code. Think of rclpy as the translator that helps Python communicate with ROS2's powerful infrastructure.

Step-by-Step: Integrating ROS2 and Python

1. **Ensure Your Virtual Environment is Active:**

   - **Action:** Before proceeding, make sure your virtual environment is activated. You should see its name in your terminal prompt.

   - **Tip:** If it's not active, run source my_robot_env/bin/activate again.

2. **Install rclpy:**

   - **Action:** Inside your virtual environment, install rclpy using pip:

```bash
pip install rclpy
```

   - **Tip:** Check the ROS2 documentation for any version-specific instructions if necessary.

3. **Create a Basic ROS2 Python Node:**

   - **Action:** Write a simple Python script that creates a ROS2 node. Open your code editor and create a file named hello_ros2.py with the following content:

```python
import rclpy
from rclpy.node import Node
```

```
class HelloRos2(Node):
    def __init__(self):
        super().__init__('hello_ros2_node')
        self.get_logger().info('Hello from ROS2
with Python!')


def main(args=None):
    rclpy.init(args=args)
    node = HelloRos2()
    rclpy.spin(node)
    node.destroy_node()
    rclpy.shutdown()


if __name__ == '__main__':
    main()
```

- o **Tip:** Save the file and run it using python hello_ros2.py to see your first **ROS2** node in action.

4. **Understand the Code:**

- o **Action:** Review the code to understand how the node is created and how ROS2's communication framework is initiated.

- o **Tip:** Notice how rclpy.init(), rclpy.spin(), and rclpy.shutdown() manage the node's lifecycle.

Tips for a Smooth Integration

- **Testing Early:**
  Run your node frequently as you develop to catch issues early.

- **Read the Documentation:**
  The ROS2 and rclpy documentation are excellent resources for understanding more complex functionality.

- **Experiment:**
  Try adding more functionality to your node gradually, such as publishing messages or subscribing to topics.

By integrating ROS2 with Python, you're equipping yourself with a flexible and powerful toolset that simplifies robotics programming.

---

6. Setting Up Your Workspace

A well-organized workspace is like a neatly arranged workshop where every tool has its place. In this section, we'll guide you through setting up a dedicated workspace for your ROS2 and Python projects.

Why a Workspace?

Workspace Benefits:

- **Organization:** Keeps all your code, configurations, and resources in one place.

- **Modularity:** Allows you to manage multiple projects without clutter.

- **Ease of Collaboration:** Makes it easier to share your work with peers or the open-source community.

Step-by-Step: Creating Your Workspace

1. **Create a Directory for Your Workspace:**

   o **Action:** Choose a location on your computer and create a new folder, for example:

```bash
mkdir -p ~/ros2_ws/src
```

   o **Tip:** The src folder is where you will place your project packages.

2. **Initialize the Workspace:**

   o **Action:** Navigate to your workspace and build it:

```bash
cd ~/ros2_ws
colcon build
```

   o **Tip:** colcon is the build tool used by ROS2. If it's not installed, follow the instructions on the ROS2 website to install it.

3. **Source the Workspace:**

- o **Action:** After building, source your workspace to ensure all environment variables are set:

bash

```
source ~/ros2_ws/install/setup.bash
```

- o **Tip:** You may add this line to your .bashrc for automatic sourcing.

4. **Create a Sample Package:**

- o **Action:** In the src directory, create a simple ROS2 package to verify your setup:

bash

```
cd ~/ros2_ws/src
ros2 pkg create --build-type ament_python
my_first_package
```

- o **Tip:** This command generates a basic package structure in Python.

Workspace Structure

Below is a diagram that represents the typical structure of a ROS2 workspace:

```
~/ros2_ws/
├── src/
│   └── my_first_package/
│       ├── package.xml
│       ├── setup.py
│       └── my_first_package/
│           └── __init__.py
└── install/ (generated after building)
```

This diagram clearly outlines the folder structure of your workspace, showing where your packages and build files reside.

Tips for an Organized Workspace

- **Consistent Naming:**
  Use clear, descriptive names for packages and files.

- **Regular Clean-Up:**
  Periodically remove temporary files and rebuild to keep the workspace tidy.

- **Documentation:**
  Maintain a README file in your workspace to track your projects and instructions.

Setting up your workspace correctly ensures that your development process remains efficient and your projects are easy to manage.

---

7. Configuring Your Tools: IDEs, Terminals, and More

Now that your workspace is set up, it's time to configure the tools that will help you code, debug, and manage your projects. The right tools can make your development process smoother and more enjoyable.

Choosing the Right IDE or Code Editor

Popular Choices:

- **Visual Studio Code (VSCode):**
  Widely used for its powerful extensions and user-friendly interface.

- **PyCharm:**
  An excellent option if you prefer a more integrated Python development environment.

- **Sublime Text:**
  Lightweight and fast, perfect for quick edits and simple projects.

Step-by-Step: Configuring Your IDE

1. **Install Your Preferred IDE:**

   o **Action:** Download and install VSCode (or your chosen IDE) from the official website.

   o **Tip:** Follow the installation wizard for your operating system.

2. **Install Essential Extensions:**

   o **Action:** For VSCode, install the following extensions:

      - Python (for Python syntax, linting, and debugging)

      - ROS (for ROS-specific features)

      - GitLens (for version control)

   o **Tip:** Extensions enhance functionality, so choose ones that best support your workflow.

3. **Configure the Terminal in Your IDE:**

   o **Action:** Set up the integrated terminal in your IDE to automatically source your ROS2 and virtual environment setups.

   o **Tip:** Modify your IDE's settings to run:

bash

```
source ~/ros2_ws/install/setup.bash
```

```
source ~/my_robot_env/bin/activate
whenever a new terminal is opened.
```

4. **Customize Your Workspace Layout:**

   - o **Action:** Organize your project folders and files within the IDE for easy navigation.

   - o **Tip:** Use workspace settings in VSCode to save your project layout, which includes file navigation, terminal configuration, and debugging settings.

Additional Tools and Tips

- **Version Control Integration:**
  Ensure Git is integrated into your IDE for seamless version control operations.

- **Debugging Tools:**
  Use the debugging features of your IDE to set breakpoints, inspect variables, and trace code execution.

- **Custom Shortcuts:**
  Configure keyboard shortcuts for common tasks to speed up your workflow.

By configuring your tools effectively, you create an environment that not only supports your coding but also enhances your productivity and creativity.

8. Testing Your Development Environment

After setting up your OS, installing ROS2, configuring Python, integrating your workspace, and fine-tuning your tools, it's time to test your development environment. Testing ensures that every component works together as expected, and it gives you the confidence to start building more complex projects.

Why Testing is Essential

Testing your environment is like doing a trial run before launching a spacecraft. It ensures that:

- **All Components Communicate Correctly:** ROS2, Python, and your tools should work in harmony.

- **No Hidden Errors Exist:** Identifying issues early prevents frustrating setbacks later.

- **You Understand the Workflow:** Familiarizing yourself with the setup builds your confidence and troubleshooting skills.

Step-by-Step: Testing Your Environment

1. **Test the ROS2 Installation:**

   - **Action:** Open two terminal windows. In one, run the talker node:

```bash
```

```
ros2 run demo_nodes_cpp talker
```

In the other, run the listener node:

```
bash
```

```
ros2 run demo_nodes_cpp listener
```

- **Tip:** If messages appear in the listener terminal, your ROS2 installation is working properly.

2. **Test Your Python Virtual Environment:**

   - **Action:** Activate your virtual environment and run a simple Python script that prints a message.

   - **Example Script:**

```python
python
```

```
print("Python virtual environment is active and
working!")
```

   - **Tip:** This simple test confirms that your Python setup and virtual environment are correctly configured.

3. **Test the ROS2 Python Node:**

   - **Action:** Run your hello_ros2.py node from the earlier step.

   - **Expected Outcome:** You should see the message "Hello from ROS2 with Python!" in your terminal.

- o **Tip:** This verifies that the integration between ROS2 and Python through rclpy is functioning as expected.

4. **Test Your Workspace Build:**

- o **Action:** Navigate to your workspace and run:

```bash

```

```
colcon build
```

- o **Tip:** Look for any errors in the build process and resolve them by following the error messages and checking your configurations.

5. **Test IDE Integration:**

- o **Action:** Open your IDE, launch the integrated terminal, and verify that the environment is correctly sourced.

- o **Tip:** Run commands like ros2 topic list or python --version to ensure the correct environments are active.

Testing Flow

Below is a diagram that outlines the testing process for your development environment:

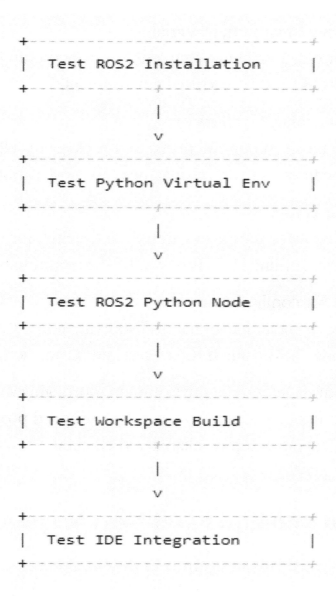

This diagram outlines a clear testing sequence, ensuring that every component of your development environment is verified and functioning correctly.

Troubleshooting Common Issues

Even the best setups can encounter issues. Here are some
tips to troubleshoot common problems:

- **Missing Environment Variables:**
  Ensure that you have sourced the correct setup files
  for ROS2 and your virtual environment.

- **Dependency Conflicts:**
  Check your requirements.txt and package installations.
  Sometimes, version mismatches can cause problems.

- **Build Errors:**
  Review error messages carefully and search for similar
  issues in online forums or the ROS2 community.

- **IDE Misconfiguration:**
  If the integrated terminal isn't sourcing correctly,
  double-check your IDE settings and startup scripts.

Testing your development environment thoroughly will give
you the confidence to move on to more advanced projects,
knowing that your setup is reliable and efficient.

---

9. Final Thoughts and Next Steps

Congratulations! By setting up your development
environment step by step, you've built the foundation for all
your future robotics projects. Remember, a robust
environment not only minimizes errors but also accelerates

your development process, letting you focus on innovation and creativity.

Reflecting on Your Setup

Take a moment to appreciate:

- **The Tools at Your Disposal:**
  You now have ROS2, Python, and a well-organized workspace ready to bring your ideas to life.

- **Your Growing Skills:**
  Each step in this setup has built your technical understanding, preparing you for the challenges ahead.

- **The Community:**
  You're part of a vibrant community of developers and enthusiasts who share your passion for robotics.

Your Next Steps

Now that your environment is ready, consider these next steps to further your learning:

- **Explore ROS2 Tutorials:**
  Delve into ROS2 tutorials to understand the core concepts of nodes, topics, services, and actions.

- **Start a Project:**
  Begin with a simple robotics project—perhaps a basic mobile robot simulation or a sensor integration experiment.

- **Engage with the Community:**
  Join forums, attend meetups, and collaborate with others to share insights and learn new techniques.

- **Keep Experimenting:**
  Don't be afraid to break things and try again. Experimentation is key to mastering robotics.

Final Encouragement

Remember, setting up your development environment is just the beginning. Each time you run a command, build a package, or run a node, you're taking another step toward mastery. Embrace the challenges, celebrate the small victories, and keep pushing your boundaries.

Rhetorical Question:
Isn't it empowering to know that your workspace is now a fully functional laboratory, ready for the next breakthrough in robotics? With each project, you not only build robots but also build confidence and skill.

Conclusion

Setting up your development environment is more than just a technical necessity—it's the launching pad for your creativity and innovation. By following this guide, you've ensured that your tools are configured correctly, your workspace is organized, and you're equipped to tackle any challenge that comes your way.

Recap of What You've Accomplished:

- **Installed Essential Software:**
  Your operating system is updated, and you've installed key tools like your terminal, IDE, Git, and other utilities.

- **Installed ROS2:**
  You now have the robust ROS2 middleware that forms the backbone of your robotics projects.

- **Set Up Python and Virtual Environments:**
  Your Python environment is isolated and ready to run powerful libraries.

- **Integrated ROS2 with Python:**
  Using rclpy, you've bridged ROS2's capabilities with Python's simplicity.

- **Organized Your Workspace:**
  A dedicated, well-structured workspace means you're ready to build and manage projects efficiently.

- **Tested Your Setup:**
  Comprehensive testing confirms that every component works together seamlessly.

- **Configured Your Tools:**
  Your IDE, terminal, and other development tools are tuned for maximum productivity.

Looking Forward

As you move forward, always remember the importance of a solid foundation. The skills you've developed in setting up your development environment will serve you well, whether you're coding your first ROS2 node or debugging a complex multi-robot system. Stay curious, stay persistent, and enjoy the journey.

Your development environment is your playground—a place where ideas turn into innovations. Keep exploring, keep experimenting, and most importantly, have fun building the future of robotics!

Chapter 3: Understanding ROS2 Fundamentals

Welcome to the world of ROS2—the Robot Operating System 2—which serves as the backbone for modern robotics software development. Whether you're building your first robotic application or looking to deepen your technical expertise, understanding ROS2 fundamentals is critical. In this chapter, we'll demystify the core concepts of ROS2 in clear, everyday language, enriched with relatable analogies, step-by-step instructions, and easy-to-follow diagrams. By the end, you'll have a strong grasp of how ROS2 works and how its components fit together to create sophisticated, responsive robotic systems.

---

1. What is ROS2? An Introduction

Imagine a bustling city where every building, vehicle, and service operates seamlessly because of a well-organized infrastructure. In robotics, ROS2 acts as that infrastructure—a set of tools, libraries, and conventions that let various parts of a robot communicate and work together harmoniously. In simple terms, ROS2 is a framework that makes it easier to develop complex robot applications by handling communication, computation, and hardware control.

Key Concepts in Plain Language

- **Modularity:** Think of ROS2 as a collection of mini-programs (called nodes) that each perform a specific task. Like different departments in a company, each node works independently yet collaborates with others.

- **Communication:** Just as citizens exchange information via phones, emails, or notice boards, ROS2 nodes talk to each other through messages. These messages are passed using well-defined channels (topics, services, and actions).

- **Flexibility:** Whether you're programming a drone, a mobile robot, or an industrial arm, ROS2 provides the flexibility to scale your project, ensuring that every piece fits perfectly.

Overview of ROS2 Components

Below is a simple diagram to illustrate the big picture:

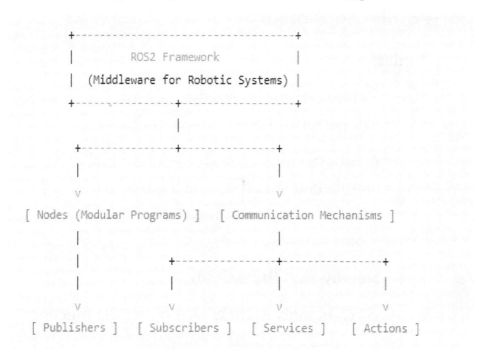

This diagram shows that ROS2 is built around nodes, which interact via publishers, subscribers, services, and actions. Each of these communication mechanisms plays a crucial role in how data and commands flow throughout your robotic system.

2. Diving into ROS2 Architecture

Now that you know what ROS2 is, let's delve into its architecture. Imagine a well-organized company where every employee has a role and every department communicates using a standardized method. ROS2's architecture is built on similar principles, ensuring that even complex systems remain manageable.

Core Building Blocks

1. **Nodes:**

   - **Definition:** Nodes are the individual processes that perform specific functions.

   - **Analogy:** Think of nodes as individual team members in an office—each has a specialized role (like sensor reading, data processing, or motor control).

   - **Step-by-Step Breakdown:**

     1. **Identify a Task:** Determine the function (e.g., reading sensor data).

     2. **Create a Node:** Write a program that performs this function.

     3. **Integrate:** Connect this node with others so they can share data.

2. **Topics:**

   - **Definition:** Topics are channels that enable nodes to exchange messages in a publish/subscribe model.

   - **Analogy:** Think of topics as bulletin boards in an office where team members post updates and notices.

- o **Usage:** One node (publisher) posts a message, and any interested node (subscriber) reads it.

3. **Services:**

   - o **Definition:** Services allow nodes to communicate synchronously—one node sends a request and waits for a response.

   - o **Analogy:** Picture calling customer service: you ask a question, and you wait for a reply.

   - o **Usage:** Ideal for tasks that require an immediate answer.

4. **Actions:**

   - o **Definition:** Actions are similar to services but are designed for tasks that take time to complete. They allow preemptible operations where progress feedback is provided.

   - o **Analogy:** Ordering a meal at a restaurant; you place your order, wait while it's prepared, and receive updates on its progress.

   - o **Usage:** Used for long-running tasks like moving a robot arm or navigating a maze.

5. **Parameters and Logging:**

   - o **Definition:** Parameters are configuration settings that allow you to customize node behavior without changing the code. Logging provides insights into node activity, similar to keeping a journal of system events.

○ **Usage:** Easily adjust settings such as sensor thresholds or motor speeds, and monitor what your nodes are doing.

ROS2 Architectural Blueprint

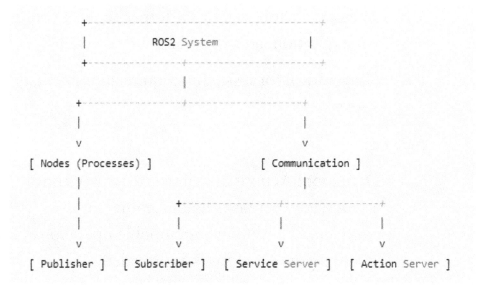

This blueprint illustrates how nodes and communication channels (publishers, subscribers, services, and actions) interconnect within ROS2, creating a powerful and flexible system.

Step-by-Step Approach to Understanding ROS2 Architecture

1. **List the Core Components:**

   - Nodes, topics, services, actions, parameters, and logging.

2. **Draw an Analogy:**

   - Imagine an office environment with employees (nodes) sharing information via bulletin boards (topics) and phone calls (services).

3. **Examine the Flow:**

   - Understand how data flows from one node to another.

4. **Visualize:**

   - Use diagrams to see the interconnections.

5. **Experiment:**

   - Create simple nodes and try connecting them using ROS2 tools.

Rhetorical Question:
Isn't it fascinating how a set of simple, well-defined components can work together to control complex machines? This modular approach is what makes ROS2 so powerful.

3. The Publisher/Subscriber Model in ROS2

One of the cornerstones of ROS2 is the publisher/subscriber model, a communication mechanism that allows nodes to exchange information effortlessly. This model is essential for creating responsive, interactive robotic systems.

What Are Publishers and Subscribers?

- **Publisher:**
    - **Role:** A node that sends out messages on a specific topic.
    - **Analogy:** Think of a publisher as someone who posts a message on a public bulletin board.

- **Subscriber:**
    - **Role:** A node that listens for messages on that same topic.
    - **Analogy:** A subscriber is like someone who regularly checks the bulletin board for updates.

Step-by-Step Process of the Publisher/Subscriber Model

1. **Set Up a Topic:**

   o **Action:** Decide on a common channel (topic) for communication.

   o **Example:** A topic called "sensor_data" for transmitting temperature readings.

2. **Create a Publisher Node:**

   o **Action:** Write a node that collects data (like temperature) and publishes it on the topic.

   o **Code Snippet (Python Example):**

```python
import rclpy
from rclpy.node import Node
from std_msgs.msg import Float32

class TemperaturePublisher(Node):
    def __init__(self):
        super().__init__('temperature_publisher')
        self.publisher_ =
self.create_publisher(Float32, 'sensor_data', 10)
        timer_period = 1.0  # seconds
```

```python
        self.timer =
self.create_timer(timer_period,
self.publish_temperature)

    def publish_temperature(self):
        msg = Float32()
        msg.data = 25.0  # Imagine this is read
from a sensor
        self.publisher_.publish(msg)
        self.get_logger().info(f'Publishing:
{msg.data}')


def main(args=None):
    rclpy.init(args=args)
    node = TemperaturePublisher()
    rclpy.spin(node)
    node.destroy_node()
    rclpy.shutdown()


if __name__ == '__main__':
    main()
```

- o **Explanation:** This code creates a publisher node that sends a temperature value every second.

3. **Create a Subscriber Node:**

   - o **Action:** Write a node that listens to the "sensor_data" topic and processes the temperature data.

o **Code Snippet (Python Example):**

```python
import rclpy
from rclpy.node import Node
from std_msgs.msg import Float32

class TemperatureSubscriber(Node):
    def __init__(self):

super().__init__('temperature_subscriber')
        self.subscription =
self.create_subscription(
            Float32,
            'sensor_data',
            self.listener_callback,
            10)
        self.subscription  # Prevent unused
variable warning

    def listener_callback(self, msg):
        self.get_logger().info(f'Received:
{msg.data}')

def main(args=None):
    rclpy.init(args=args)
    node = TemperatureSubscriber()
    rclpy.spin(node)
```

```
node.destroy_node()
rclpy.shutdown()


if __name__ == '__main__':
    main()
```

- ○ **Explanation:** This subscriber node listens to the same topic and logs the received data.

4. **Test the Communication:**

   - ○ **Action:** Run both nodes in separate terminal windows to observe the data flow.

   - ○ **Tip:** Verify that the subscriber receives the published messages.

Why This Model Works

- **Decoupling of Components:**
  Publishers and subscribers do not need to know about each other directly. This separation allows for easier maintenance and scalability.

- **Real-Time Data Flow:**
  The model ensures that data is transmitted in near real-time, which is essential for responsive robotics applications.

- **Simplicity and Flexibility:**
  Whether you're dealing with sensor data, control commands, or any other type of information, this model adapts seamlessly.

Rhetorical Question:

Can you imagine how much easier your projects become when you can add or remove components without disrupting the entire system? That's the magic of the publisher/subscriber model in ROS2.

---

4. Services and Actions: Synchronous and Asynchronous Communication

While the publisher/subscriber model is excellent for continuous data exchange, some scenarios require a request-and-response interaction. This is where services and actions come into play.

Understanding Services

Services in ROS2 allow nodes to communicate synchronously. One node sends a request, and another node responds. This is ideal for operations that require an immediate answer.

- **Analogy:**
  Think of a service as making a phone call to get a specific piece of information—like calling a colleague to ask for the latest report.

- **Step-by-Step Example:**

  1. **Create a Service Server:**

- Write a node that offers a service (e.g., providing the current battery status).

2. **Create a Service Client:**

- Write a node that sends a request to the server and waits for the response.

3. **Test the Interaction:**

- Run both nodes and verify that the client receives the expected data.

Understanding Actions

Actions are designed for tasks that take longer to complete. Unlike services, actions allow for feedback and can be preempted if necessary.

- **Analogy:**
  Imagine ordering a pizza. You place the order (send a goal), receive periodic updates (feedback), and eventually, the pizza is delivered (result). If you change your mind, you can cancel the order.

- **Step-by-Step Example:**

  1. **Define an Action:**

     - Create an action definition that outlines the goal, feedback, and result.

  2. **Implement an Action Server:**

- Write a node that executes the action, such as moving a robot arm to a specified position.

3. **Implement an Action Client:**

- Write a node that sends a goal to the action server and listens for feedback.

4. **Test the Interaction:**

- Verify that the action client receives feedback and a final result.

Services and Actions Communication Flow

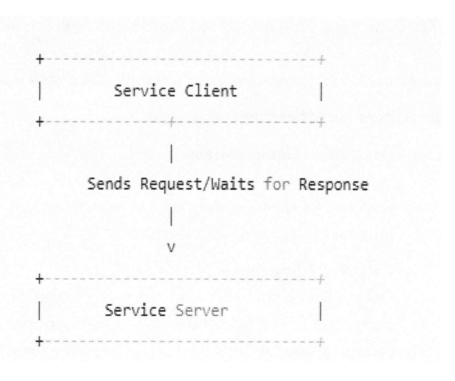

For Actions:

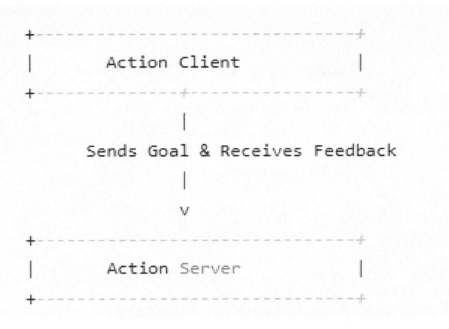

These diagrams illustrate the two distinct communication patterns in ROS2—one for immediate responses (services) and another for long-running tasks with feedback (actions).

Benefits of Using Services and Actions

- **Precision in Communication:**
  Services ensure you get an immediate, reliable response for queries, while actions let you monitor progress on tasks that take time.

- **Enhanced Flexibility:**
  Depending on your task requirements, you can choose between synchronous and asynchronous communication without altering the overall system architecture.

- **Improved Control:**
  Actions provide the ability to cancel or preempt long-running tasks, which is invaluable in dynamic robotic applications.

Rhetorical Question:
Wouldn't it be amazing to have both quick, on-demand responses and detailed progress reports for more complex operations? That's exactly what services and actions offer in ROS2.

5. Working with ROS2 Parameters and Logging

Beyond basic communication, managing configuration settings and monitoring system behavior are crucial parts of developing reliable robotics applications. ROS2 parameters and logging mechanisms help you achieve this.

Parameters: Configuring Your Nodes

Parameters in ROS2 let you define settings that control how nodes behave. Instead of hardcoding values in your program, parameters allow you to adjust configurations on the fly.

- **Analogy:**
  Think of parameters as the settings on your smartphone—brightness, volume, and connectivity

options that you can change without needing to rewrite the entire operating system.

- **Step-by-Step:**

    1. **Declare Parameters in Your Node:**

        - When initializing a node, declare the parameters that it will use.

    2. **Set Default Values:**

        - Provide default values for these parameters.

    3. **Modify Parameters at Runtime:**

        - Use ROS2 tools to change parameter values without restarting the node.

    4. **Access Parameters in Code:**

        - Retrieve the parameter values during runtime to alter node behavior dynamically.

Logging: Keeping Track of Your System

Logging in ROS2 provides a way to monitor and record the behavior of nodes. It's similar to keeping a detailed diary of system events, which can be invaluable for debugging and performance tuning.

- **Step-by-Step:**

    1. **Integrate Logging Statements:**

- Insert logging commands at key points in your node's code.

2. **Categorize Logs:**

   - Use different logging levels (**INFO, WARN, ERROR**) to classify messages.

3. **Review Logs:**

   - Monitor logs in the terminal or using external tools to understand node performance and behavior.

4. **Adjust Logging Levels:**

   - Change the verbosity of logs based on your debugging needs.

Parameters and Logging Workflow

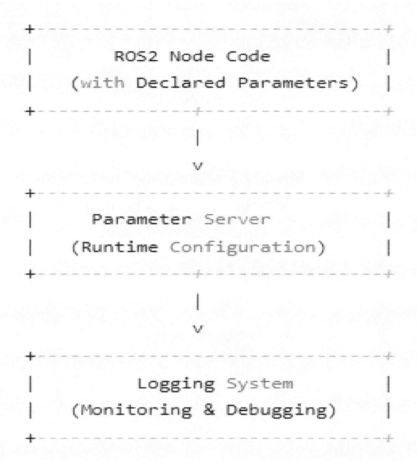

```
+------------------------------------------------+
|              ROS2 Node Code                    |
|       (with Declared Parameters)               |
+------------------------------------------------+

                      |
                      v

+------------------------------------------------+
|            Parameter Server                    |
|        (Runtime Configuration)                 |
+------------------------------------------------+

                      |
                      v

+------------------------------------------------+
|              Logging System                    |
|         (Monitoring & Debugging)               |
+------------------------------------------------+
```

This diagram shows how parameters and logging integrate with your node, allowing for dynamic configuration and effective monitoring.

Best Practices for Parameters and Logging

- **Keep Parameters Modular:**
  Group related parameters together to maintain clarity.

- **Use Meaningful Names:**
  Name your parameters and log messages in a way that clearly indicates their purpose.

- **Log Strategically:**
  Insert logging statements where they can provide the most insight—such as before and after critical operations.

- **Monitor Continuously:**
  Regularly check your logs to preemptively catch issues before they become major problems.

Rhetorical Question:
How much easier would troubleshooting be if you could adjust settings on the fly and have a clear record of system events at your fingertips? With parameters and logging, ROS2 makes this possible.

---

6. Advanced ROS2 Communication Patterns

Once you've mastered the basics, you can explore more advanced communication patterns in ROS2. These patterns are designed for high-performance and complex robotic systems where timing, concurrency, and data integrity are crucial.

Executors: Managing Concurrency

Executors in ROS2 manage the execution of nodes, especially when dealing with asynchronous callbacks. They are responsible for scheduling and handling multiple tasks concurrently.

- **Analogy:**
  Think of an executor as a project manager who oversees multiple teams (nodes) working on different tasks. The manager ensures that each team gets the resources it needs at the right time.

- **Step-by-Step:**

  1. **Choose an Executor Type:**

     - ROS2 offers single-threaded and multi-threaded executors. Decide which one fits your application.

  2. **Implement the Executor:**

     - Integrate the executor into your code to handle callbacks efficiently.

  3. **Test Concurrency:**

     - Validate that your system handles multiple tasks without lag or data loss.

Lifecycle Nodes: Managing Node States

Lifecycle nodes allow you to manage a node's state, from initialization to shutdown, in a controlled manner. They provide a way to gracefully handle transitions and ensure that nodes are only active when needed.

- **Step-by-Step:**

  1. **Define Lifecycle Callbacks:**

     - Implement callbacks for different states (e.g., configuring, activating, shutting down).

  2. **Monitor Transitions:**

     - Use ROS2 tools to observe the state changes of your lifecycle nodes.

  3. **Adjust Behavior:**

     - Ensure your node performs the correct actions during state transitions.

Advanced Communication Patterns

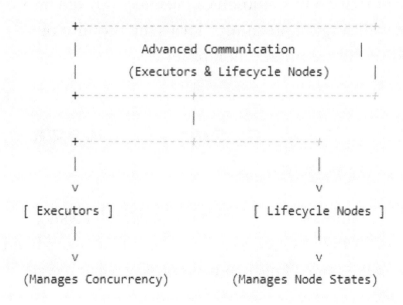

```
+-------------------------------------------------+
|              Advanced Communication             |
|           (Executors & Lifecycle Nodes)         |
+-----------------------+-------------------------+
                        |
+-----------------------+-------------------------+
|                                       |
v                                       v
[ Executors ]                    [ Lifecycle Nodes ]
     |                                  |
     v                                  v
(Manages Concurrency)            (Manages Node States)
```

This diagram illustrates how advanced mechanisms like executors and lifecycle nodes enhance ROS2's communication capabilities.

Benefits of Advanced Patterns

- **Improved Performance:**
  Executors enable efficient management of multiple concurrent tasks.

- **Controlled Node Behavior:**
  Lifecycle nodes ensure that nodes transition smoothly between different states.

- **Robust Systems:**
  These patterns are essential in high-demand scenarios, such as autonomous vehicles or industrial automation.

Rhetorical Question:
Can you imagine the power of a system where every component is not only communicating effectively but also managed with surgical precision? That's the promise of advanced ROS2 communication patterns.

---

7. Putting It All Together: Building a Simple ROS2 Node

Now that you understand the fundamentals and advanced concepts of ROS2, it's time to roll up your sleeves and build a simple ROS2 node. This hands-on project will integrate what you've learned so far—from creating nodes to setting up communication.

Step-by-Step Guide to Building a Simple Node

1. **Set Up Your Environment:**

    o **Action:** Ensure that ROS2 and your Python virtual environment are active.

    o **Tip:** Double-check that you have sourced the ROS2 setup files.

2. **Create a New Node Package:**

    o **Action:** Use the ROS2 command-line tool to create a package.

```bash
bash
```

```
ros2 pkg create --build-type ament_python
simple_node_package
```

    o **Tip:** This command creates a directory with the basic structure for your package.

3. **Write the Node Code:**

    o **Action:** Open the generated Python file and implement a simple node that publishes a greeting message.

    o **Code Example:**

```python
python
```

```python
import rclpy
from rclpy.node import Node
from std_msgs.msg import String


class GreetingPublisher(Node):
    def __init__(self):
        super().__init__('greeting_publisher')
        self.publisher_ =
self.create_publisher(String, 'greetings', 10)
        self.timer = self.create_timer(2.0,
self.publish_greeting)

    def publish_greeting(self):
        msg = String()
        msg.data = "Hello from your ROS2 node!"
        self.publisher_.publish(msg)
        self.get_logger().info(f'Published:
{msg.data}')


def main(args=None):
    rclpy.init(args=args)
    node = GreetingPublisher()
    rclpy.spin(node)
    node.destroy_node()
    rclpy.shutdown()


if __name__ == '__main__':
```

```
main()
```

- o **Explanation:** This node publishes a greeting every two seconds on the topic "greetings."

4. **Build and Run the Node:**

- o **Action:** Navigate to your workspace and build the package:

```bash
bash
```

```bash
colcon build --packages-select
simple_node_package
```

- o **Test:** Source the workspace and run the node:

```bash
bash
```

```bash
source install/setup.bash
ros2 run simple_node_package greeting_publisher
```

5. **Observe the Output:**

- o **Action:** Open another terminal and subscribe to the "greetings" topic:

```bash
bash
```

```bash
ros2 topic echo /greetings
```

- o **Tip:** Verify that you see the greeting messages being published.

Learning Outcomes

By completing this project, you have:

- Integrated key ROS2 concepts into a working node.

- Practiced creating, building, and running ROS2 packages.

- Seen firsthand how nodes communicate via topics.

Rhetorical Question:
Doesn't it feel rewarding to see your code come alive, broadcasting messages that could one day control a real robot? Every line of code brings you closer to mastering robotics.

---

8. Troubleshooting and Best Practices in ROS2

Even the best setups can face challenges. Here, we cover common pitfalls in ROS2 development and offer actionable tips to overcome them.

Common Issues and Their Solutions

1. **Missing or Incorrectly Sourced Environment Variables:**

   o **Issue:** ROS2 commands not recognized.

   o **Solution:** Always source the ROS2 setup file in every new terminal:

bash

```
source /opt/ros/<distro>/setup.bash
```

2. **Dependency Conflicts:**

   o **Issue:** Package build failures due to version mismatches.

   o **Solution:** Verify your dependencies in the package configuration and use virtual environments to isolate installations.

3. **Communication Failures:**

   o **Issue:** Subscribers not receiving messages.

   o **Solution:** Ensure that the topic names match exactly between publishers and subscribers, and check network settings if using distributed systems.

4. **Performance Bottlenecks:**

   o **Issue:** Nodes lagging or missing messages.

   o **Solution:** Consider using multi-threaded executors and optimize callback functions.

Step-by-Step Troubleshooting Approach

1. **Verify Environment Setup:**

   o Confirm that all necessary setup files are sourced.

2. **Check Logs:**

- o Use ROS2's logging tools to inspect error messages.

3. **Isolate Components:**

   - o Test individual nodes before integrating them into larger systems.

4. **Consult Documentation:**

   - o Refer to ROS2 documentation and community forums for similar issues.

5. **Iterate and Test:**

   - o Make incremental changes and test frequently.

Best Practices for a Smooth ROS2 Experience

- **Modularize Your Code:**
  Keep each node focused on a single task to simplify debugging.

- **Maintain Clear Naming Conventions:**
  Consistent topic names, parameter names, and node identifiers reduce confusion.

- **Use Version Control:**
  Track changes using Git to roll back to known good states.

- **Regularly Test Components:**
  Verify that each node and communication channel works independently before integrating them.

- **Engage with the Community:**
  Leverage forums, Q&A sites, and official ROS2
  channels for support.

Rhetorical Question:

Isn't it much easier to navigate challenges when you have a
systematic approach and a set of best practices guiding you?
With these strategies, you're well-equipped to tackle any
obstacle in your ROS2 journey.

---

9. Conclusion: Mastering the ROS2 Fundamentals

Congratulations on completing this deep dive into the
fundamentals of ROS2! We started by breaking down what
ROS2 is and why it's a game-changer in robotics. We
explored its architecture, learning how nodes, topics,
services, and actions form the building blocks of modern
robotic systems. You've seen how the publisher/subscriber
model enables continuous data flow, while services and
actions provide the structure for on-demand and long-
running tasks.

We also covered essential tools like parameters and logging,
which give you control over your node configurations and
help you monitor system performance. Advanced topics,
such as executors and lifecycle nodes, demonstrated how
ROS2 scales to meet the demands of complex applications.
Finally, by building a simple ROS2 node, you put theory

into practice—transforming abstract concepts into a tangible, working example.

Reflecting on Your Journey

- **From Theory to Practice:**
  You've moved from understanding the theory behind ROS2 to implementing your own nodes, witnessing firsthand how communication flows between components.

- **Empowered by Knowledge:**
  With these fundamentals in hand, you're ready to take on more advanced projects and explore new horizons in robotics.

- **A Community of Innovators:**
  Remember that ROS2 is supported by a vibrant community. Engage with peers, contribute to discussions, and never stop learning.

Final Words of Encouragement

Every robotics expert started with the basics—much like the foundations of a building. By mastering ROS2 fundamentals, you have laid a solid groundwork that will support your future innovations. Whether you dream of building autonomous vehicles, service robots, or industrial automation systems, the skills you've acquired here are indispensable.

Rhetorical Question:

Are you ready to transform your ideas into reality, leveraging the power of ROS2 to create robotic systems that can change the world? The journey is challenging but incredibly rewarding, and your deep understanding of these fundamentals is the key to unlocking endless possibilities.

In Summary

In this chapter, we covered:

- **What is ROS2?**
  An introduction to the framework that powers modern robotic applications.

- **ROS2 Architecture:**
  A look at nodes, topics, services, actions, parameters, and logging, explained with everyday analogies.

- **Publisher/Subscriber Model:**
  Detailed, step-by-step guidance on how nodes communicate through topics.

- **Services and Actions:**
  A breakdown of synchronous and asynchronous communication, complete with relatable examples.

- **Parameters and Logging:**
  How to configure your nodes and monitor their behavior in real time.

- **Advanced Communication Patterns:**
  An exploration of executors and lifecycle nodes for high-performance systems.

- **Building a Simple Node:**
  A practical project that brings all these concepts together.

- **Troubleshooting and Best Practices:**
  A systematic approach to solving common issues and optimizing your ROS2 development workflow.

By integrating clear explanations, relatable analogies, actionable steps, and easy-to-understand diagrams, this chapter aims to empower you with a comprehensive understanding of ROS2 fundamentals. Each section builds on the previous one without repetition, ensuring that every new concept adds unique value to your learning journey.

Your Next Steps

Now that you have a strong grasp of ROS2 fundamentals, here are some next steps to continue your exploration:

1. **Experiment Further:**

   - Try modifying the example nodes provided in this chapter. Change parameters, add more topics, or even implement a new service.

2. **Join the Community:**

- o Participate in ROS2 forums, attend webinars, and join local robotics meetups to exchange ideas and get support.

3. **Advance Your Knowledge:**

- o Explore advanced tutorials, integrate more complex sensors, and experiment with multi-node communication setups.

4. **Apply Your Skills:**

- o Start a project that addresses a real-world problem. Whether it's building a home automation robot or designing a simulation for an industrial process, applying what you've learned will solidify your expertise.

Final Reflective Thought:
Every breakthrough in robotics begins with a single step. With your newfound understanding of ROS2, you're now well-equipped to take that next leap into innovation. Embrace the challenges, celebrate your progress, and keep pushing the boundaries of what's possible.

Chapter 4: Python Essentials for Robotics

Welcome to the world of Python for robotics—a realm where code meets creativity to bring robots to life! In this chapter, we'll explore the Python language from a robotics perspective. We'll cover everything from basic syntax and core data structures to essential libraries and best practices. Whether you're just starting out or looking to sharpen your skills, this guide will provide you with a solid foundation to develop robust and innovative robotics applications using Python.

Throughout this chapter, you'll find clear, jargon-free explanations, relatable analogies, step-by-step instructions, and helpful diagrams that simplify even the most complex workflows. So, grab your virtual toolbox and let's dive into the essentials that make Python such a powerful language for robotics.

1. Introduction: The Role of Python in Robotics

Imagine you're a chef with a kitchen full of ingredients. Python is like your favorite set of kitchen tools—versatile, easy to use, and capable of turning raw data into a gourmet meal. In robotics, Python serves as the backbone for rapid development, quick prototyping, and even complex data processing tasks.

Why Python for Robotics?

- **Simplicity and Readability:**
  Python's syntax is designed to be clear and straightforward. This means you can write and understand code faster, reducing the time it takes to bring your robotic ideas to life.

- **Extensive Library Support:**
  From numerical computing with NumPy to data visualization with Matplotlib and image processing with OpenCV, Python's rich ecosystem of libraries makes it a one-stop solution for many robotics challenges.

- **Community and Resources:**
  With a massive global community, you have access to countless tutorials, forums, and projects that can help you overcome obstacles and spark new ideas.

- **Rapid Prototyping:**
  Python enables you to quickly build prototypes, test algorithms, and iterate on designs without getting bogged down by complex syntax.

Rhetorical Question:
Have you ever wished you could focus more on innovating with your robot rather than wrestling with convoluted code? Python is here to make that dream a reality!

2. Python Basics for Robotics

Before we start building sophisticated robotic systems, let's revisit the fundamentals of Python. Think of these basics as the building blocks of a house; without a solid foundation, even the most advanced designs will crumble. In this section, we'll cover the key elements of Python programming that are especially relevant to robotics.

2.1 Understanding Syntax and Variables

At its core, Python is a high-level, interpreted language that emphasizes readability. Let's break down some of the basic components:

Variables and Data Types

Variables are like labeled jars where you store your ingredients—in this case, data. Python supports several data types:

- **Integers and Floats:**
  Numbers such as 3 (integer) or 3.14 (float) are used in calculations, like determining the speed or distance a robot must travel.

- **Strings:**
  Sequences of characters used to store text. For instance, you might use a string to label different parts of your robot.

- **Booleans:**
  Represent True or False values, which are essential for decision-making in control loops.

- **Lists and Tuples:**
  Ordered collections of items. Lists (e.g., [1, 2, 3]) are mutable, meaning you can change them, while tuples (e.g., (1, 2, 3)) are immutable.

Step-by-Step: Declaring Variables

1. **Choose a Descriptive Name:**
   Instead of x = 10, use motor_speed = 10 to make your code more readable.

2. **Assign a Value:**
   Simply use the assignment operator (=) to store a value.

3. **Use Variables in Operations:**
   For example, total_distance = motor_speed * time_elapsed.

Example Code:

```python
python


# Define a motor speed (in RPM) and a time
duration (in seconds)
motor_speed = 120        # RPM
time_elapsed = 5         # seconds
```

```
# Calculate distance (assume a direct
proportionality for simplicity)
distance_traveled = motor_speed * time_elapsed
print("Distance traveled:", distance_traveled)
```

2.2 Control Structures and Functions

Control structures let you direct the flow of your program, much like the traffic signals in a busy city. They help your robot make decisions based on sensor data and conditions.

If-Else Statements

These are used for decision-making. For example, if a sensor detects an obstacle, the robot must stop or change direction.

Example:

```python
obstacle_detected = True

if obstacle_detected:
    print("Stopping the robot.")
else:
    print("Continuing forward.")
```

Loops

Loops are essential for repetitive tasks, such as reading sensor data continuously or iterating over a list of commands.

For Loop Example:

python

```python
# Loop through a list of sensor values
sensor_readings = [0.5, 1.2, 0.9, 1.5]
for reading in sensor_readings:
    print("Sensor reading:", reading)
```

While Loop Example:

python

```python
# Use a while loop to simulate continuous
monitoring
counter = 0
while counter < 5:
    print("Monitoring sensors...")
    counter += 1
```

Functions

Functions help encapsulate code into reusable blocks. Think of functions as mini-programs that perform a specific task, such as processing sensor data or controlling a motor.

Example Function:

python

```python
def calculate_distance(speed, time):
    """Calculate the distance traveled given
speed and time."""
```

```
    return speed * time


distance = calculate_distance(120, 5)
print("Calculated distance:", distance)
```

2.3 Data Structures and Their Uses in Robotics

Data structures are the containers that hold and organize your data. In robotics, managing data efficiently is critical for performance and real-time processing.

Lists and Dictionaries

- **Lists:**
  Used for ordered collections. They are perfect for storing sensor data streams, commands, or waypoints for navigation.

Example:

```python
python


waypoints = [(0, 0), (1, 2), (3, 4)]
for point in waypoints:
    print("Waypoint:", point)
```

- **Dictionaries:**
  Allow you to store data in key-value pairs. They're

useful for configuration settings or mapping sensor IDs to their readings.

Example:

```python
sensor_values = {"front": 1.2, "left": 0.8,
"right": 1.0}
for sensor, value in sensor_values.items():
    print(f"Sensor {sensor} reading: {value}")
```

Tuples and Sets

- **Tuples:**
  Immutable sequences, useful for fixed data like coordinate pairs.

- **Sets:**
  Collections of unique elements, ideal for ensuring no duplicate sensor IDs or error codes.

Python Data Structures in Robotics

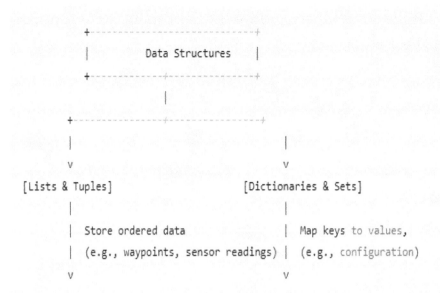

This diagram shows how different data structures serve unique purposes in organizing and managing data in robotics applications.

---

3. Essential Python Libraries for Robotics

Now that you're comfortable with Python basics, it's time to explore the powerful libraries that bring your robotic projects to life. Python's extensive ecosystem allows you to perform complex computations, visualize data, and interface with hardware—all with just a few lines of code.

3.1 NumPy: The Engine for Numerical Computation

What is NumPy?

NumPy is a library for numerical computing. It provides support for arrays, matrices, and a wide range of mathematical functions. In robotics, NumPy is indispensable for tasks like sensor data analysis, image processing, and controlling motion.

Step-by-Step: Using NumPy

1. **Install NumPy:**

    o Use pip:

bash

```
pip install numpy
```

2. **Import and Create Arrays:**

python

```
import numpy as np
# Create a 1D array of sensor values
sensor_data = np.array([0.5, 1.2, 0.9, 1.5])
print("Sensor Data:", sensor_data)
```

3. **Perform Operations:**

    o NumPy allows you to perform element-wise operations, which is especially useful for filtering and transforming sensor data.

```python
python
```

```python
# Increase all sensor readings by 10%
adjusted_data = sensor_data * 1.10
print("Adjusted Sensor Data:", adjusted_data)
```

3.2 Matplotlib: Visualizing Your Data

What is Matplotlib?

Matplotlib is a plotting library that helps you visualize data. In robotics, visualizations can help you debug sensor readings, analyze performance, or simply understand how your robot is performing in real time.

Step-by-Step: Creating a Plot

1. **Install Matplotlib:**

   o Use pip:

```bash
bash
```

```bash
pip install matplotlib
```

2. **Import and Plot Data:**

```python
python
```

```python
import matplotlib.pyplot as plt
import numpy as np

# Create sample data
time = np.linspace(0, 10, 100)
```

```
sensor_readings = np.sin(time)

# Plot the sensor readings over time
plt.plot(time, sensor_readings, label="Sensor
Data")
plt.xlabel("Time (s)")
plt.ylabel("Sensor Reading")
plt.title("Sensor Data Over Time")
plt.legend()
plt.show()
```

3.3 OpenCV: Computer Vision for Robotics

What is OpenCV?

OpenCV is a library focused on computer vision tasks. It's widely used in robotics for object detection, image processing, and visual feedback.

Step-by-Step: Basic Image Processing with OpenCV

1. **Install OpenCV:**

   o Use pip:

```bash
```

```
pip install opencv-python
```

2. **Import and Process an Image:**

```python
```

```
import cv2
```

```
# Read an image from file
image = cv2.imread('robot_view.jpg')
# Convert to grayscale
gray_image = cv2.cvtColor(image,
cv2.COLOR_BGR2GRAY)
# Display the image
cv2.imshow('Grayscale Image', gray_image)
cv2.waitKey(0)
cv2.destroyAllWindows()
```

3.4 Other Useful Libraries

While NumPy, Matplotlib, and OpenCV are among the most popular, there are other libraries that can be extremely useful in robotics:

- **PySerial:**
  For communicating with hardware over serial ports—essential when interfacing with sensors or microcontrollers.

- **SciPy:**
  Builds on NumPy for advanced mathematical functions, including optimization and signal processing.

- **Pandas:**
  Though primarily used in data analysis, Pandas can help manage large datasets from robot sensors.

Python Libraries Ecosystem in Robotics

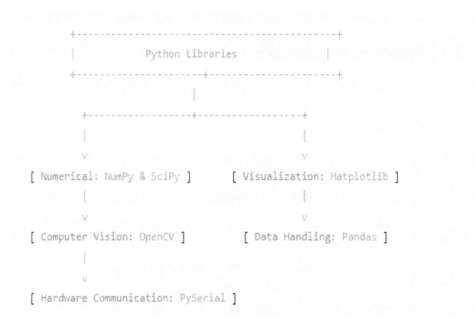

```
            +------------------------------------------+
            |            Python Libraries              |
            +----------------------+-------------------+
                                   |
            +------------------+------------------+
            |                                     |
            v                                     v
  [ Numerical: NumPy & SciPy ]      [ Visualization: Matplotlib ]
            |                                     |
            v                                     v
  [ Computer Vision: OpenCV ]        [ Data Handling: Pandas ]
            |
            v
  [ Hardware Communication: PySerial ]
```

This diagram provides an overview of how different Python libraries support various aspects of robotics development.

---

4. Best Practices in Python for Robotics

As you build more complex robotics projects, writing clean, efficient, and maintainable code becomes critical. Here, we discuss best practices that help you keep your Python code professional and robust.

4.1 Code Readability and Organization

- **Follow PEP8 Guidelines:**
  Python's style guide, PEP8, helps ensure that your

code is consistent and easy to read. Use proper indentation, meaningful variable names, and spacing.

- **Modularize Your Code:**
  Break your code into functions and modules. This makes it easier to test individual components and reuse code across projects.

- **Document Your Code:**
  Use comments and docstrings to explain what your code does. Think of this as writing a user manual for your robot's brain.

Step-by-Step: Writing Readable Code

1. **Indentation:**

   o Use 4 spaces per indentation level.

2. **Comments:**

   o Write comments above complex sections of code.

3. **Function Documentation:**

   o Use triple-quoted strings to document functions.

Example:

```python

def calculate_velocity(distance, time):
    """
```

```
    Calculate the velocity given distance and
time.

    Parameters:
    - distance (float): Distance traveled (in
meters)
    - time (float): Time taken (in seconds)

    Returns:
    - float: Velocity (in meters per second)
    """
    if time == 0:
        return 0
    return distance / time
```

4.2 Error Handling and Debugging Techniques

No code is perfect on the first try—especially when working on complex robotics systems. Effective error handling and debugging are your best friends.

- **Use Try-Except Blocks:**
  Catch and handle exceptions gracefully to prevent your program from crashing.

- **Logging:**
  Incorporate logging to record runtime information, which can be invaluable for troubleshooting.

- **Interactive Debugging:**
  Use tools like pdb (Python Debugger) to step through your code and inspect variables.

Example:

```python
python


import logging


def safe_divide(a, b):
    try:
        return a / b
    except ZeroDivisionError:
        logging.error("Attempted to divide by
zero!")
        return None


result = safe_divide(10, 0)
print("Result:", result)
```

4.3 Virtual Environments and Dependency Management

Keeping your project's dependencies organized is crucial. Virtual environments allow you to isolate your Python packages for each project, preventing conflicts and making your code more reproducible.

Step-by-Step: Setting Up a Virtual Environment

1. Install Virtualenv (if needed):

bash

```
pip install virtualenv
```

2. Create a New Environment:

bash

```
python -m venv robotics_env
```

3. Activate the Environment:

- On Linux/macOS:

bash

```
source robotics_env/bin/activate
```

- On Windows:

bash

```
robotics_env\Scripts\activate
```

4. Install Required Libraries:

bash

```
pip install numpy matplotlib opencv-python
```

5. Building a Simple Python-Based Robot Simulation

Now that you have the essentials down, it's time to put theory into practice. In this section, we'll build a simple robot simulation using Python. This project will help you understand how to integrate sensor data, simulate movement, and visualize results.

5.1 Project Overview

Imagine you want to simulate a robot that navigates a room while avoiding obstacles. We'll create a basic simulation where the robot:

- Generates random sensor data.

- Processes this data to decide whether to move forward or turn.

- Visualizes its path on a simple 2D plot.

5.2 Setting Up the Project

Step-by-Step:

1. **Create a Project Directory:**

bash

```
mkdir robot_simulation
cd robot_simulation
```

2. **Set Up a Virtual Environment:**

```bash
bash
```

```bash
python -m venv sim_env
source sim_env/bin/activate
```

3. **Install Required Libraries:**

```bash
bash
```

```bash
pip install numpy matplotlib
```

5.3 Writing the Simulation Code

Let's build the simulation step by step.

Step 1: Import Libraries and Initialize Parameters

```python
python
```

```python
import numpy as np
import matplotlib.pyplot as plt


# Simulation parameters
num_steps = 100
step_size = 1.0  # Distance per step
room_size = (20, 20)  # Dimensions of the room
(width, height)
```

Step 2: Simulate Robot Movement

We'll simulate the robot's movement by generating random angles for each step. The robot will adjust its position based on the step size and direction.

```python

# Initialize the robot's starting position at the
center of the room
position = np.array([room_size[0] / 2,
room_size[1] / 2])
positions = [position.()]


# Simulate movement for a given number of steps
for _ in range(num_steps):
    # Generate a random direction (angle in
radians)
    angle = np.random.uniform(0, 2 * np.pi)
    # Calculate movement vector
    movement = step_size *
np.array([np.cos(angle), np.sin(angle)])
    # Update the position
    position = position + movement
    # Keep the robot within the room bounds
    position = np.clip(position, [0, 0],
room_size)
    positions.append(position.())
```

Step 3: Visualize the Robot's Path

Now, we'll plot the robot's path using Matplotlib.

```python

positions = np.array(positions)
```

```
plt.figure(figsize=(8, 8))
plt.plot(positions[:, 0], positions[:, 1],
marker='o', linestyle='-')
plt.title("Robot Simulation: Path Visualization")
plt.xlabel("X Position")
plt.ylabel("Y Position")
plt.xlim(0, room_size[0])
plt.ylim(0, room_size[1])
plt.grid(True)
plt.show()
```

5.4 Running and Testing Your Simulation

After writing your simulation code:

- **Run the Script:**
  Execute your Python file in the terminal.

- **Observe the Output:**
  A window should open displaying the path of the robot. The plot will show how the robot moves within the defined room.

- **Experiment:**
  Modify parameters like num_steps, step_size, and room_size to see how the simulation changes.

Rhetorical Question:
Doesn't it feel amazing to see your code come alive in a visual simulation? This project is a great stepping stone toward more advanced robotics simulations.

6. Integrating Python with Hardware

While simulations are a fantastic way to prototype, real-world robotics involves interacting with physical hardware. Python's flexibility extends to hardware integration, allowing you to control sensors, actuators, and even microcontrollers.

6.1 Communicating with Sensors and Actuators

Imagine you want your robot to read data from a distance sensor and control a motor based on that data. Python can interface with hardware through various libraries.

Example: Using PySerial to Communicate with a Microcontroller

1. **Install PySerial:**

bash

```
pip install pyserial
```

2. **Basic Code to Read from a Serial Port:**

python

```
import serial

# Open the serial port (adjust 'COM3' or
'/dev/ttyUSB0' as needed)
```

```
ser = serial.Serial('COM3', 9600, timeout=1)


def read_sensor_data():
    line = ser.readline().decode('utf-
8').rstrip()
    return line


while True:
    data = read_sensor_data()
    if data:
        print("Sensor Data:", data)
```

Note: This code reads sensor data from a serial port and prints it. In a real robotics application, you'd process this data to make decisions.

6.2 Using GPIO Libraries (Raspberry Pi Example)

For those using Raspberry Pi or similar platforms, controlling hardware directly through GPIO pins is common.

1. **Install RPi.GPIO (for Raspberry Pi):**

```bash
pip install RPi.GPIO
```

2. **Example: Controlling an LED**

```python
```

```python
import RPi.GPIO as GPIO
import time

# Set up GPIO using BCM numbering
GPIO.setmode(GPIO.BCM)
LED_PIN = 18
GPIO.setup(LED_PIN, GPIO.OUT)

# Blink the LED
try:
    while True:
        GPIO.output(LED_PIN, GPIO.HIGH)
        time.sleep(1)
        GPIO.output(LED_PIN, GPIO.LOW)
        time.sleep(1)
except KeyboardInterrupt:
    GPIO.cleanup()
```

Rhetorical Question:

Isn't it thrilling to know that with just a few lines of Python, you can control real-world hardware? This is the bridge between simulation and tangible robotics.

7. Advanced Python Techniques in Robotics

Once you've mastered the basics, it's time to explore more advanced Python techniques that can take your robotics projects to the next level.

7.1 Asynchronous Programming and Concurrency

In robotics, handling multiple tasks concurrently is often necessary. Python's asyncio library provides a way to write asynchronous code that can manage multiple operations without blocking.

Step-by-Step: Asynchronous Programming Example

1. **Import the asyncio Module:**

python

```python
import asyncio
```

2. **Define an Asynchronous Function:**

python

```python
async def read_sensor():
    await asyncio.sleep(1)  # Simulate sensor
read delay
    return "Sensor value: 42"
```

```
async def main():
    sensor_value = await read_sensor()
    print(sensor_value)
```

```
asyncio.run(main())
```

This example demonstrates how asynchronous functions allow your robot to perform tasks like reading sensor data without halting other processes.

7.2 Integrating Machine Learning into Robotics

Python's machine learning libraries, such as TensorFlow and PyTorch, open up new possibilities in robotics. From object recognition to path planning, integrating ML can make your robot smarter.

Step-by-Step: Simple Machine Learning Integration

1. **Install TensorFlow:**

```bash
```

```
pip install tensorflow
```

2. **Example: Predicting Sensor Data Trends**

```python
```

```
import numpy as np
import tensorflow as tf
from tensorflow import keras
```

```python
# Create dummy sensor data
X = np.array([[i] for i in range(100)])
y = np.array([2 * i + 1 for i in range(100)])


# Build a simple linear regression model
model = keras.Sequential([
    keras.layers.Dense(units=1, input_shape=[1])
])


model.compile(optimizer='sgd',
loss='mean_squared_error')
model.fit(X, y, epochs=50)


# Predict a new value
prediction = model.predict([[100]])
print("Predicted value for sensor reading 100:", prediction)
```

Rhetorical Question:
Imagine a robot that learns from its environment—adapting to changes and making informed decisions. Python's machine learning capabilities make this possible!

Machine Learning Integration in Robotics

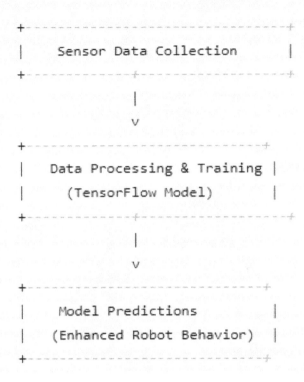

```
+-----------------------------------+
|       Sensor Data Collection      |
+-----------------+-----------------+
                  |
                  v
+-----------------------------------+
|      Data Processing & Training    |
|        (TensorFlow Model)          |
+-----------------+-----------------+
                  |
                  v
+-----------------------------------+
|         Model Predictions          |
|     (Enhanced Robot Behavior)      |
+-----------------------------------+
```

This diagram shows how raw sensor data can be transformed into intelligent behavior through machine learning.

7.3 Multithreading for Performance

Python's multithreading and multiprocessing modules can help you optimize performance when handling resource-intensive tasks.

Example Using Multithreading:

python

```
import threading
import time
```

```python
def task(name):
    for i in range(5):
        print(f"Task {name}: iteration {i}")
        time.sleep(1)


# Create threads for simultaneous tasks
thread1 = threading.Thread(target=task,
args=("A",))
thread2 = threading.Thread(target=task,
args=("B",))


thread1.start()
thread2.start()


thread1.join()
thread2.join()
print("Both tasks completed.")
```

This example shows how you can run multiple tasks in parallel, a technique that is particularly useful when your robot must perform sensor processing and control operations concurrently.

---

8. Conclusion and Next Steps

Congratulations! You've now journeyed through the essential aspects of Python for robotics—from the basics of syntax and data structures to advanced techniques like asynchronous programming and machine learning integration. Let's recap the key takeaways and explore your next steps.

Recap of Key Concepts

- **Python Fundamentals:**
  You've learned about variables, control structures, functions, and data structures, all of which are the building blocks of any robotics application.

- **Essential Libraries:**
  Libraries such as NumPy, Matplotlib, and OpenCV empower you to perform numerical computations, visualize data, and process images—crucial tasks in robotics.

- **Best Practices:**
  Writing clean, modular code, handling errors gracefully, and using virtual environments ensure your projects remain scalable and maintainable.

- **Practical Projects:**
  Building a simple robot simulation and integrating Python with hardware demonstrated how theory transforms into real-world applications.

- **Advanced Techniques:**
  Asynchronous programming, machine learning integration, and multithreading open up possibilities for creating smarter, more responsive robotic systems.

Your Next Steps

1. **Deepen Your Knowledge:**

   o Experiment with different libraries and frameworks.

   o Explore advanced topics like reinforcement learning or deep neural networks for robotics.

2. **Apply What You've Learned:**

   o Start a project that interests you—whether it's a robot that navigates a maze, performs object detection, or interacts with users.

   o Share your code on platforms like GitHub to collaborate with others.

3. **Join the Community:**

   o Participate in online forums, local robotics meetups, and hackathons.

   o Engage with peers to exchange ideas, troubleshoot issues, and learn new techniques.

4. **Keep Experimenting:**

   o Tinker with your simulations.

   o Integrate Python with hardware and explore real-time data processing.

Rhetorical Question:
Isn't it empowering to know that you now have the tools and

knowledge to turn your robotic ideas into reality? With Python as your ally, the possibilities are as limitless as your imagination.

Final Words of Encouragement

Every expert was once a beginner. The journey of mastering Python for robotics is filled with experimentation, challenges, and breakthroughs. Celebrate your progress and continue to build, test, and refine your projects. Remember, every line of code brings you one step closer to creating the next innovative robotic solution.

Visualize Your Future:
Picture yourself developing robots that not only perform tasks but also learn, adapt, and interact intelligently with the world. With Python in your toolkit, you're well-equipped to drive the future of robotics.

In Summary

This chapter has taken you on a comprehensive journey through Python essentials for robotics. We covered:

- **Fundamental Concepts:**
  From syntax and variables to control structures and functions.

- **Data Structures:**
  How lists, dictionaries, tuples, and sets help manage the flow of data in your applications.

- **Essential Libraries:**
  Leveraging NumPy for numerical tasks, Matplotlib for visualization, and OpenCV for computer vision.

- **Best Practices:**
  Writing readable, maintainable code with proper error handling and using virtual environments.

- **Practical Simulation:**
  Building a simple robot simulation to see Python in action.

- **Hardware Integration:**
  Communicating with sensors and actuators using PySerial and GPIO libraries.

- **Advanced Techniques:**
  Asynchronous programming, multithreading, and machine learning integration for smarter robotics.

Each section has provided actionable insights and step-by-step guidance, ensuring that every concept is not only understood but ready to be applied in your own robotics projects.

Final Reflective Thought:
Just as a master craftsman hones their tools over years of practice, your journey with Python for robotics is a continuous process of learning and innovation. With every new project, you'll find more efficient ways to solve

problems, more creative ways to integrate technology, and more reasons to be excited about the future of robotics.

So, what will you build next?

Happy coding, and may your robotic creations continue to push the boundaries of what's possible with Python

Chapter 5: Building Your First Robot Simulation

Welcome to the exciting world of robot simulation—a realm where virtual prototypes come to life before they ever touch real hardware. In this chapter, we're going to walk through the process of building your very first robot simulation, step by step. Whether you're a hobbyist eager to test your ideas or a professional looking to refine complex behaviors, simulation is an essential tool for validating your concepts, debugging your designs, and ultimately, saving time and resources before investing in physical prototypes.

By the end of this chapter, you'll have a clear understanding of what a robot simulation entails, how to plan your simulation project, and how to build, run, and refine a simulation using accessible tools. Along the way, we'll break down technical concepts into clear, jargon-free language, use relatable analogies, and provide actionable steps with diagrams and code snippets that make even the most complex ideas easy to grasp.

1. Introduction: Why Simulate Before You Build?

Imagine planning a road trip without consulting a map or GPS—you might end up lost or face unexpected obstacles along the way. Building a robot without first simulating its behavior is much the same. Simulation acts as your virtual proving ground, allowing you to test and tweak your robot's performance in a controlled environment. It's a safe space to experiment, learn, and innovate without the risk of damaging expensive hardware or compromising safety.

Key Benefits of Simulation:

- **Risk Reduction:**
  Identify and fix potential issues before they become costly mistakes in the real world.

- **Rapid Iteration:**
  Make adjustments on the fly without the need to rebuild or reconfigure physical components.

- **Cost Efficiency:**
  Save money on materials and labor by validating concepts virtually.

- **Performance Analysis:**
  Gather data and insights into how your robot behaves under various conditions.

Rhetorical Question:
Have you ever wished you could test drive a car before buying it? Simulation gives you that test-drive experience— allowing you to perfect your robot's performance long before the rubber meets the road.

2. Planning Your Simulation Project

Before you start coding, it's crucial to plan your simulation project as meticulously as you'd plan a construction project. Think of this phase as drafting blueprints before building a house. A well-laid plan will help you set clear objectives, choose the right tools, and define the scope of your simulation.

2.1 Define Your Objectives

Begin by asking yourself: **What do I want my robot to do?** Your objectives will drive the design of your simulation. For example, you might want your robot to:

- Navigate a cluttered environment.

- Follow a predetermined path.

- Avoid obstacles and reach a target location.

- Manipulate objects or interact with its surroundings.

Action Steps:

1. **Write Down Your Goals:**

    o Example: "I want my robot to autonomously navigate a maze while avoiding obstacles."

2. **Determine the Key Features:**

    o What sensors will it need? (e.g., distance sensors, cameras)

- o What control algorithms will be involved? (e.g., path planning, obstacle avoidance)

3. **Set Success Criteria:**

- o Define measurable outcomes such as "The robot should complete the maze in under 2 minutes without collisions."

2.2 Identify the Tools and Software

To simulate your robot, you'll need a set of tools. Common choices include:

- **Simulation Platforms:**
  Tools like Gazebo, Webots, or even custom Python-based simulators offer rich environments for testing robot behavior.

- **Programming Frameworks:**
  Since you're already familiar with Python and ROS2 from earlier chapters, we'll leverage these to integrate simulation with our control code.

- **Modeling Tools:**
  For creating robot models, you may use URDF (Unified Robot Description Format) files or SDF (Simulation Description Format) files.

Planning Your Simulation Project

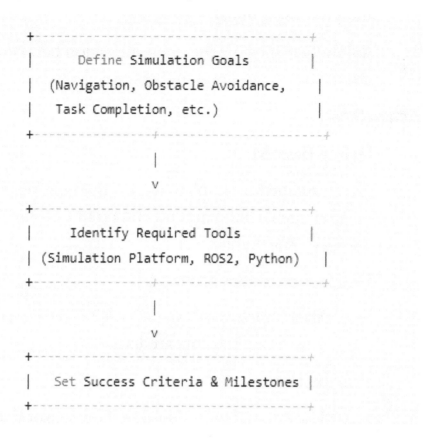

```
+----------------------------------------+
|        Define Simulation Goals         |
|    (Navigation, Obstacle Avoidance,    |
|     Task Completion, etc.)             |
+----------------------------------------+
                    |
                    v
+----------------------------------------+
|          Identify Required Tools       |
|   (Simulation Platform, ROS2, Python)  |
+----------------------------------------+
                    |
                    v
+----------------------------------------+
|   Set Success Criteria & Milestones    |
+----------------------------------------+
```

This diagram lays out the high-level steps in planning your simulation project, ensuring that every decision is aligned with your overall objectives.

2.3 Sketch Out a High-Level Design

Before diving into code, create a rough sketch of your simulation's architecture. This could include:

- A layout of the simulated environment (e.g., a maze or room with obstacles).

- A diagram of the robot's design (its sensors, actuators, and processing units).

- A flowchart showing the communication between simulation components and control algorithms.

Action Steps:

1. **Draw a Basic Map:**

   o Outline the simulation area, marking key elements like start and end points, obstacles, and waypoints.

2. **Design Your Robot Model:**

   o Sketch the robot's shape and indicate where sensors and motors are located.

3. **Plan the Data Flow:**

   o Use a flowchart to illustrate how sensor data is collected, processed, and used to make navigation decisions.

Rhetorical Question:
Wouldn't it be easier to build a machine if you had a detailed blueprint to follow? Your high-level design serves as that blueprint, guiding your development process.

3. Setting Up the Simulation Environment

With your plan in hand, it's time to set up your simulation environment—the digital playground where your robot will come to life. In this section, we'll focus on configuring your simulation tools, ensuring that your virtual environment is as close as possible to the real world.

3.1 Choosing a Simulation Platform

There are several excellent simulation platforms available, but for this project, we'll use **Gazebo**—a robust, open-source simulation tool that integrates seamlessly with ROS2. Gazebo provides realistic physics, dynamic environments, and a wealth of plugins to simulate sensors and actuators.

Action Steps:

1. **Download and Install Gazebo:**

   - Follow the official installation guide for your operating system.

   - On Ubuntu, for example, you might run:

```bash
bash
```

```bash
sudo apt update
sudo apt install gazebo11
```

2. **Integrate Gazebo with ROS2:**

o Make sure you have the appropriate ROS2 packages installed that enable Gazebo integration.

o Test the integration by launching a sample Gazebo simulation:

bash

```
ros2 launch gazebo_ros gazebo.launch.py
```

3. **Explore the Gazebo Interface:**

o Familiarize yourself with the interface, learn how to add objects, and understand basic controls like camera manipulation and simulation time.

3.2 Configuring the Simulation Workspace

Your simulation workspace is where you'll organize all the files and configurations related to your project. This includes your robot's model files (URDF/SDF), world files for Gazebo, and any ROS2 launch files that control the simulation.

Action Steps:

1. **Create a Dedicated Workspace:**

o Set up a directory structure that separates your simulation files from your control code.

o Example:

bash

```
mkdir -p ~/robot_sim_ws/src
cd ~/robot_sim_ws/src
```

2. Organize Your Files:

- Create subdirectories for models, worlds, and launch files.

- Example structure:

```bash
```

```
~/robot_sim_ws/
    ├──── src/
    /       ├──── models/
    /       ├──── worlds/
    /       └──── launch/
    └──── install/
```

3. Version Control:

- Initialize a Git repository in your workspace to track changes and collaborate with others.

- Example:

```bash
```

```
cd ~/robot_sim_ws
git init
```

Simulation Workspace Structure

This diagram provides a clear visual of how to organize your simulation workspace, making it easier to manage and maintain.

---

4. Designing Your Robot Model

A key element of any robot simulation is the digital representation of your robot. This model defines the robot's physical properties, sensor placements, and joints. We'll use URDF (Unified Robot Description Format) for this purpose—a powerful yet straightforward XML-based format that describes your robot's structure.

4.1 Understanding URDF Basics

URDF files define your robot as a collection of links (representing rigid bodies) and joints (representing connections between links). Think of it as a blueprint that outlines every component of your robot, from its base to its arms, sensors, and wheels.

Key Concepts:

- **Links:**
  Represent parts of the robot, such as the chassis, wheels, or sensor mounts.

- **Joints:**
  Define how links are connected. Joints can be fixed, revolute (rotational), or prismatic (sliding).

Action Steps:

1. **Familiarize Yourself with URDF Syntax:**

   o Read a simple URDF example to understand the XML structure.

2. **Outline Your Robot's Structure:**

   o Sketch your robot on paper, marking key links and joints.

3. **Write a Basic URDF File:**

   o Start by defining a simple robot with a base and two wheels.

Example URDF Snippet:

```xml
<robot name="simple_robot">
  <link name="base_link">
    <visual>
      <geometry>
```

```xml
        <box size="1 0.5 0.2"/>
      </geometry>
      <material name="blue"/>
    </visual>
  </link>
  <link name="wheel_left">
    <visual>
      <geometry>
        <cylinder length="0.1" radius="0.2"/>
      </geometry>
      <material name="black"/>
    </visual>
  </link>
  <link name="wheel_right">
    <visual>
      <geometry>
        <cylinder length="0.1" radius="0.2"/>
      </geometry>
      <material name="black"/>
    </visual>
  </link>
  <joint name="left_wheel_joint"
type="continuous">
    <parent link="base_link"/>
    <child link="wheel_left"/>
    <origin xyz="-0.5 0.3 0" rpy="0 0 0"/>
    <axis xyz="0 1 0"/>
  </joint>
```

```
    <joint name="right_wheel_joint"
type="continuous">

    <parent link="base_link"/>

    <child link="wheel_right"/>

    <origin xyz="-0.5 -0.3 0" rpy="0 0 0"/>

    <axis xyz="0 1 0"/>

  </joint>

</robot>
```

Rhetorical Question:

Wouldn't it be great to see your robot's design take shape on the screen before you even begin coding its behavior? A well-crafted URDF file is the first step in making that vision a reality.

4.2 Visualizing Your Robot Model

After creating your URDF file, you can use tools like **RViz** or Gazebo's built-in model viewer to see your robot in action. This step is crucial for verifying that your model's dimensions, joint placements, and sensor locations are accurate.

Action Steps:

1. **Launch RViz:**

   o Use a ROS2 launch file to load your URDF model into RViz.

2. **Inspect the Model:**

- o Check that all components are correctly positioned and oriented.

3. **Make Adjustments:**

- o Refine the URDF file based on your observations and repeat the visualization process until you're satisfied.

---

5. Integrating Simulation with ROS2 and Python

With your robot model ready and your simulation environment set up, it's time to integrate everything using ROS2 and Python. This integration lets you control your simulated robot just as you would a real one, using ROS2 nodes and Python scripts.

5.1 Creating a Control Node

The control node is the brain of your simulation. It sends commands to your robot, processes sensor data, and makes decisions in real time.

Step-by-Step:

1. **Create a ROS2 Package for Your Control Code:**

bash

```
ros2 pkg create --build-type ament_python
robot_control
```

2. **Write a Python Node:**

   - Create a file named control_node.py inside the package.

   - Use ROS2's rclpy library to set up a basic node that, for example, publishes velocity commands.

Example Code:

```python
python


import rclpy
from rclpy.node import Node
from geometry_msgs.msg import Twist


class RobotControl(Node):
    def __init__(self):
        super().__init__('robot_control')
        self.publisher_ =
self.create_publisher(Twist, 'cmd_vel', 10)
        self.timer = self.create_timer(0.5,
self.send_command)

    def send_command(self):
        msg = Twist()
        # Simple logic: move forward at constant
speed
        msg.linear.x = 0.5
        msg.angular.z = 0.0
        self.publisher_.publish(msg)
```

```
        self.get_logger().info("Publishing
velocity command")


def main(args=None):
    rclpy.init(args=args)
    node = RobotControl()
    rclpy.spin(node)
    node.destroy_node()
    rclpy.shutdown()


if __name__ == '__main__':
    main()
```

3. **Launch the Node:**

   - Create a ROS2 launch file to start your control node along with the simulation environment.

   - This ensures that your simulation and control logic run in harmony.

---

6. Creating a Simulation Scenario

A simulation is not just about a robot moving in an empty space—it's about creating scenarios that mimic real-world challenges. In this section, we'll build a simulation scenario where your robot must navigate through a cluttered environment.

6.1 Designing the Environment

Start by defining the layout of your simulated world. This could be a maze, a room with obstacles, or an open field with dynamic elements.

Action Steps:

1. **Create a World File:**

   o Use SDF (Simulation Description Format) or a Gazebo world file to define the environment.

   o Include elements like walls, obstacles, and target locations.

Example World Snippet (SDF):

xml

```xml
<sdf version="1.6">
  <world name="obstacle_world">
    <include>
      <uri>model://ground_plane</uri>
    </include>
    <include>
      <uri>model://sun</uri>
    </include>
    <!-- Define obstacles -->
    <model name="obstacle1">
      <static>true</static>
      <link name="link">
```

```
<visual name="visual">
  <geometry>
    <box>
      <size>1 1 1</size>
    </box>
  </geometry>
</visual>
</link>
<pose>2 2 0.5 0 0 0</pose>
</model>
</world>
</sdf>
```

2. **Place Your Robot:**

   o Define the initial position of your robot in the world file.

   o Ensure it's positioned at a logical starting point relative to obstacles.

6.2 Programming Robot Behavior for Navigation

Your robot needs logic to navigate through the environment. This can include:

- **Obstacle Avoidance:**
  Use sensor data (simulated or virtual) to detect obstacles and adjust course.

- **Path Planning:**
  Implement simple algorithms to steer your robot toward a goal.

Action Steps:

1. **Implement Sensor Simulation:**

   - Create a Python node that simulates sensor readings (e.g., distance to obstacles).

   - Use these readings to trigger behavior changes.

2. **Add Decision-Making Logic:**

   - Within your control node, add conditions that change the robot's velocity or direction based on sensor input.

Example Logic (Pseudo-Code):

```python
python


if sensor_reading < threshold:
    # Obstacle detected, turn left
    msg.linear.x = 0.0
    msg.angular.z = 0.5
else:
    # Clear path, move forward
    msg.linear.x = 0.5
    msg.angular.z = 0.0
```

3. **Test the Behavior:**

- o Run the simulation and observe how the robot reacts to obstacles.

- o Tweak thresholds and timing to optimize performance.

Navigation Decision Flowchart

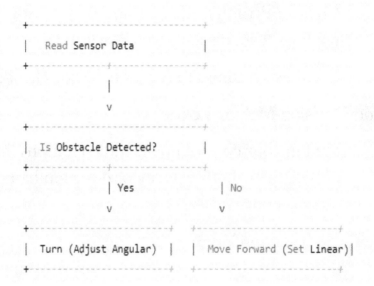

```
+--------------------------------------+
|   Read Sensor Data                   |
+------------------+-------------------+
                   |
                   v
+--------------------------------------+
|  Is Obstacle Detected?               |
+------------------+-------------------+
                   | Yes              | No
                   v                  v
+------------------------+  +---------------------------+
|  Turn (Adjust Angular) |  |  Move Forward (Set Linear)|
+------------------------+  +---------------------------+
```

This flowchart captures the simple decision-making process for obstacle avoidance in your simulation.

7. Running and Debugging Your Simulation

With your environment configured, robot model integrated, and control logic in place, it's time to run your simulation. As with any complex system, debugging is an integral part of the process. This section will guide you through launching your simulation, monitoring its behavior, and troubleshooting common issues.

7.1 Launching the Simulation

Step-by-Step:

1. **Launch the Simulation Environment:**

   o Use your ROS2 launch files to start Gazebo with your world file and robot model.

   o Example command:

```bash
ros2 launch my_simulation launch_simulation.py
```

2. **Start Your Control Node:**

   o In a separate terminal, launch your Python control node.

   o Verify that both the simulation and control nodes are running concurrently.

3. **Monitor Outputs:**

   o Use ROS2 tools like ros2 topic echo to monitor topics (e.g., sensor data, velocity commands).

   o Use RViz or Gazebo's interface to visually inspect the robot's behavior.

7.2 Debugging Common Issues

When things don't go as planned, systematic troubleshooting is key.

Troubleshooting Checklist:

- **Check Environment Variables:**

  o Ensure that ROS2 and Gazebo setup files are sourced correctly.

- **Verify Topic Connections:**

  o Use commands like ros2 topic list to confirm that all expected topics are active.

- **Examine Logs:**

  o Look at console outputs and log messages for error clues.

- **Isolate Components:**

  o Test individual nodes (e.g., run the control node in isolation) to identify the source of issues.

- **Adjust Simulation Parameters:**

  o If the robot behaves erratically, consider tweaking sensor thresholds or update frequencies.

8. Analyzing Simulation Data

Simulation isn't just about watching your robot move—it's also about gathering data to understand its performance. In this section, we'll discuss how to log, visualize, and analyze simulation data to refine your robot's behavior.

8.1 Logging Data

Record relevant metrics such as:

- Sensor readings over time.

- Velocity commands.

- Collision events or near-misses.

Action Steps:

1. **Incorporate Logging in Your Code:**

    o Use ROS2's built-in logging utilities to print and store important data.

2. **Save Logs to Files:**

    o Configure your nodes to write logs to a file for later analysis.

8.2 Visualizing Data with Python

Use libraries like Matplotlib to plot simulation data. Visualizations help you quickly identify trends or issues.

Example Code:

```python
```

```
import matplotlib.pyplot as plt
import numpy as np

# Example: Simulated sensor readings over time
time_steps = np.linspace(0, 10, 100)
sensor_values = np.sin(time_steps) +
np.random.normal(0, 0.1, 100)

plt.figure(figsize=(10, 5))
plt.plot(time_steps, sensor_values, label="Sensor
Readings")
plt.xlabel("Time (s)")
plt.ylabel("Sensor Value")
plt.title("Simulated Sensor Data Over Time")
plt.legend()
plt.show()
```

9. Enhancing and Expanding Your Simulation

Once your basic simulation is up and running, the next step is to enhance it by adding more features and refining performance. This is where creativity meets technical expertise, allowing you to push the boundaries of what your simulation can do.

9.1 Adding More Sensors and Actuators

Consider simulating additional sensors such as cameras, LIDAR, or ultrasonic sensors to provide richer data. Similarly, add actuators like robotic arms or grippers to simulate complex interactions.

Action Steps:

1. **Modify Your Robot Model:**

   o Update your URDF file to include new sensor links.

2. **Integrate Sensor Data:**

   o Develop ROS2 nodes that simulate and process data from these sensors.

3. **Test and Validate:**

   o Run the simulation and ensure that the new components behave as expected.

9.2 Implementing Advanced Control Algorithms

Once your simulation environment is stable, experiment with more sophisticated algorithms:

- **Path Planning:**
  Implement algorithms such as A^* or Dijkstra's algorithm to optimize navigation.

- **Machine Learning:**
  Integrate basic ML models to predict sensor data or optimize control strategies.

- **Dynamic Environment Interaction:**
  Simulate moving obstacles or environmental changes to test your robot's adaptability.

9.3 Optimizing Performance

Performance is critical, especially in simulations that mimic real-time operation. Here are some best practices:

- **Optimize Code:**
  Refactor your Python scripts to reduce latency and improve efficiency.

- **Adjust Simulation Parameters:**
  Tweak update rates and physics engine settings in Gazebo for smoother performance.

- **Profile and Monitor:**
  Use profiling tools to identify bottlenecks and resolve them.

Rhetorical Question:
Wouldn't it be satisfying to see your simulation run smoothly and efficiently, reflecting the true potential of your robot's design? Continuous optimization is key to achieving that level of performance.

10. Conclusion: From Simulation to Real-World Impact

Congratulations on building your first robot simulation! You've journeyed through planning, designing, integrating, and refining a complete simulation environment—a powerful tool that not only saves time and resources but also sharpens your engineering skills.

10.1 Recap of Key Steps

- **Planning:**
  You defined your objectives, selected tools, and drafted a high-level design.

- **Environment Setup:**
  You set up Gazebo, organized your workspace, and integrated it with ROS2.

- **Robot Modeling:**
  You created and refined a URDF model to represent your robot.

- **Control Integration:**
  You built a Python control node that communicates with your simulation.

- **Scenario Creation:**
  You designed an environment complete with obstacles and navigation challenges.

- **Running and Debugging:**
  You launched your simulation, monitored its performance, and troubleshooted issues.

- **Data Analysis:**
  You collected and visualized data to understand your robot's behavior.

- **Enhancements:**
  You learned how to expand and optimize your simulation for advanced functionalities.

10.2 Your Journey Forward

The simulation you've built is just the beginning. With these skills in your arsenal, you can now explore more complex scenarios, integrate real sensor data, and eventually transition from simulation to physical implementation. Every simulation you build is a step toward more innovative, resilient, and intelligent robotic systems.

Final Reflective Thought:
Have you ever watched a flight simulator and felt the thrill of piloting an aircraft from the safety of your home? That's the power of simulation—transforming ideas into virtual reality, so you're ready when it's time to take flight in the real world.

11. Final Words of Encouragement

Building a robot simulation is a transformative experience. Not only do you gain technical expertise, but you also cultivate a mindset of iterative development and continuous improvement. Every bug you squash and every behavior you fine-tune brings you closer to creating robots that can navigate, interact, and perform in the real world.

Remember, simulation is more than just a testing ground—it's a creative space where you can experiment freely, learn from mistakes, and push the boundaries of what's possible. Embrace the process, celebrate your progress, and don't be afraid to try new approaches. Your simulated robot today could be the blueprint for a revolutionary design tomorrow.

Rhetorical Question:
Are you ready to take your ideas from the digital realm into the physical world, confident in the knowledge that every simulation is a stepping stone toward real-world innovation?

In Summary

In this comprehensive chapter, we've covered:

- **The Importance of Simulation:**
  Why testing virtually is crucial before committing to real hardware.

- **Planning Your Project:**
  Defining objectives, choosing tools, and sketching a high-level design.

- **Setting Up the Environment:**
  Installing and configuring Gazebo, integrating with ROS2, and organizing your workspace.

- **Designing the Robot Model:**
  Creating a URDF file, visualizing your robot, and refining its design.

- **Integrating ROS2 and Python:**
  Developing control nodes and linking them to your simulation environment.

- **Creating a Simulation Scenario:**
  Designing an environment with obstacles, implementing navigation logic, and testing behavior.

- **Running, Debugging, and Analyzing:**
  Launching your simulation, troubleshooting issues, and using data analysis to refine performance.

- **Enhancing Your Simulation:**
  Adding new sensors, implementing advanced algorithms, and optimizing for real-time performance.

Each section was designed to be clear, actionable, and free of unnecessary jargon—so you can focus on building something truly innovative.

12. Your Next Steps: From Virtual to Reality

Now that you've built your first robot simulation, consider these next steps to further your journey:

1. **Iterate and Experiment:**

   o Tweak your simulation parameters, try different navigation algorithms, or add new environmental challenges.

2. **Integrate Real Hardware:**

   o Transition from simulation to a physical prototype by connecting real sensors and actuators.

3. **Collaborate and Share:**

   o Publish your simulation code on GitHub, join online robotics forums, and collaborate with peers to refine your designs.

4. **Advance Your Skills:**

   o Explore advanced simulation topics such as multi-robot systems, reinforcement learning for autonomous navigation, or sensor fusion techniques.

5. **Document Your Journey:**

    o   Keep a detailed log of your experiments, successes, and challenges. This documentation can serve as a valuable resource for future projects and for sharing with the robotics community.

Rhetorical Question:

Isn't it exhilarating to think that what started as a virtual simulation can eventually transform into a real, working robot that makes an impact in the world? Your journey from simulation to reality is just beginning.

---

13. Final Reflection

Building your first robot simulation is more than just a technical exercise—it's a gateway to endless possibilities. With a robust simulation in place, you're equipped to test, refine, and ultimately bring to life the robotic innovations of tomorrow. Every step you take in this digital playground builds your confidence, sharpens your skills, and fuels your creativity.

So, take a deep breath, hit that "Run" button, and watch as your simulated robot navigates a world you've designed. Enjoy every moment of this process, and remember: every great invention starts with a simple simulation.

Happy simulating, and here's to a future where your robotic creations not only work flawlessly in virtual environments but also revolutionize the real world!

Chapter 6: Advanced Robotics Concepts

Welcome to the next frontier in robotics—a realm where creativity meets cutting-edge technology to solve complex problems. In this chapter, we'll dive into advanced robotics concepts that push the boundaries of what robots can achieve. Whether you're an experienced roboticist or a curious enthusiast ready to level up, this guide will demystify sophisticated techniques and present them in clear, actionable steps. We'll explore topics like advanced navigation, control algorithms, multi-robot coordination, sensor fusion, artificial intelligence integration, and human-robot interaction. Get ready to transform your ideas into innovations that can reshape industries and improve lives.

Rhetorical Question:
Have you ever wondered how self-driving cars weave through traffic with precision or how warehouse robots coordinate seamlessly in large fleets? The secrets lie in advanced robotics concepts—tools that let us design systems with intelligence, adaptability, and reliability.

---

1. Advanced Navigation and SLAM

Navigating in complex environments is one of the most challenging tasks for a robot. Advanced navigation techniques, particularly SLAM (Simultaneous Localization and Mapping), are essential for robots to understand and interact with their surroundings in real time.

1.1 What is SLAM?

SLAM is the process by which a robot builds a map of an unknown environment while simultaneously tracking its own location within that map. Imagine you're in a dark room with only a flashlight. As you move around, you not only avoid obstacles but also gradually form a mental map of the room. That's essentially what SLAM enables a robot to do.

Key Concepts in SLAM:

- **Localization:**
  Determining the robot's position within a known map.

- **Mapping:**
  Creating a map of the environment from sensor data.

- **Data Association:**
  Matching new sensor readings to previously mapped features.

1.2 Step-by-Step SLAM Process

1. **Collect Sensor Data:**

   o Gather data using sensors such as LIDAR, cameras, or ultrasonic sensors.

2. **Feature Extraction:**

- o Identify key features (edges, corners, landmarks) in the environment.

3. **Data Association:**

- o Match these features with existing map elements.

4. **Localization:**

- o Estimate the robot's position relative to the map.

5. **Mapping Update:**

- o Incorporate new data to refine the map.

6. **Loop Closure:**

- o Detect when the robot revisits a location and adjust the map to correct errors.

Actionable Tips:

- Use well-calibrated sensors to improve accuracy.

- Implement filtering techniques (e.g., Kalman Filters, Particle Filters) to smooth data.

- Test your SLAM algorithm in controlled environments before deploying in dynamic settings.

Rhetorical Question:
Can you imagine the power of a robot that learns its environment on the fly, continuously refining its internal map while navigating through a bustling city? That's the promise of SLAM.

2. Advanced Control Algorithms

Once your robot knows where it is and what its environment looks like, the next challenge is to control its movement with precision. Advanced control algorithms ensure that your robot responds effectively to dynamic conditions, maintains stability, and performs tasks with accuracy.

2.1 Understanding Control Systems

At their core, control systems are like the steering and braking mechanisms in a car—they adjust actions based on feedback to achieve the desired outcome. In robotics, control algorithms govern everything from motor speeds to joint angles.

Key Components:

- **Feedback Loop:**
  Continuously monitors the robot's state and adjusts control signals.

- **PID Control:**
  A popular control strategy that uses Proportional, Integral, and Derivative terms to minimize error.

- **Model Predictive Control (MPC):**
  A more advanced method that predicts future states and optimizes control inputs accordingly.

- **Robust Control:**
Ensures stability in the presence of uncertainties and external disturbances.

2.2 Step-by-Step: Implementing a PID Controller

1. **Define the Setpoint:**

   o Determine the target value for the system (e.g., desired motor speed).

2. **Measure the Process Variable:**

   o Collect real-time data from sensors (e.g., current speed).

3. **Calculate the Error:**

   o Error = Setpoint – Process Variable.

4. **Compute the PID Terms:**

   o **Proportional (P):** Directly proportional to the error.

   o **Integral (I):** Accumulates past errors.

   o **Derivative (D):** Predicts future error trends.

5. **Generate the Control Signal:**

   o Combine the PID terms to form the output.

6. **Apply the Control Signal:**

   o Send the output to the actuators (e.g., motors).

Actionable Tips:

- Start with tuning the proportional term, then add integral and derivative terms gradually.

- Use simulation tools to test and refine your controller before deploying on physical hardware.

- Consider implementing anti-windup strategies to manage integral accumulation.

Rhetorical Question:
Imagine steering a boat through turbulent waters—precise adjustments at every moment are crucial to stay on course. That's exactly what advanced control algorithms do for your robot.

---

3. Multi-Robot Systems and Coordination

In today's interconnected world, many robotics applications involve not just a single robot but a fleet of robots working in unison. Multi-robot systems (MRS) open up exciting possibilities in areas like warehouse automation, search and rescue, and agricultural monitoring.

3.1 Why Multi-Robot Systems?

Multi-robot systems can collaborate to complete tasks more efficiently than individual robots working alone. Think of it as a well-coordinated team where each member has a role, and together they achieve more than the sum of their parts.

Key Benefits:

- **Increased Efficiency:**
  Robots can divide tasks and cover more ground.

- **Redundancy and Robustness:**
  If one robot fails, others can take over, ensuring the mission continues.

- **Scalability:**
  Multi-robot systems can be scaled up to handle larger, more complex tasks.

3.2 Step-by-Step: Implementing Multi-Robot Coordination

1. **Define Communication Protocols:**

   o Establish how robots will share information (e.g., using ROS2 topics or services).

2. **Assign Roles:**

   o Determine the tasks for each robot (e.g., exploration, data collection, obstacle clearing).

3. **Develop Coordination Algorithms:**

   o Implement algorithms such as consensus algorithms or behavior-based control to synchronize actions.

4. **Test Inter-Robot Communication:**

   o Use simulation to verify that robots can exchange data and respond to each other's actions.

5. **Implement Collision Avoidance:**

   o Incorporate safety protocols to prevent robots from colliding with each other.

Actionable Tips:

- Start small: Begin with a pair of robots and gradually increase the number.

- Use simulations to identify bottlenecks and communication delays.

- Explore swarm robotics techniques for large-scale applications.

3.3 Multi-Robot Communication Network

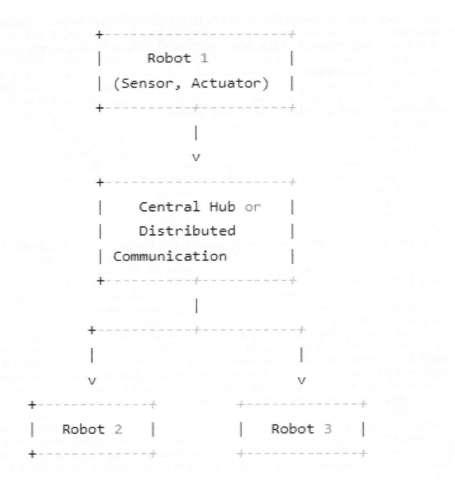

```
+----------------------+
|       Robot 1        |
|  (Sensor, Actuator)  |
+----------+-----------+
           |
           v
+----------------------+
|    Central Hub or    |
|     Distributed      |
|    Communication     |
+----------+-----------+
           |
+----------+-----------+
|                      |
v                      v
+-------------+    +---------------+
|  Robot 2    |    |   Robot 3     |
+-------------+    +---------------+
```

This diagram shows a simplified view of how multiple robots can communicate through a central hub or a distributed network, enabling coordinated actions.

Rhetorical Question:
Imagine a flock of birds moving in perfect harmony—each bird adjusts its flight based on its neighbors, creating mesmerizing patterns. That's the essence of multi-robot coordination.

4. Artificial Intelligence and Machine Learning in Robotics

Incorporating artificial intelligence (AI) and machine learning (ML) into robotics is revolutionizing how machines perceive, learn, and act. These technologies empower robots with the ability to make decisions, recognize patterns, and adapt to new situations in ways that traditional programming cannot match.

4.1 The Role of AI in Robotics

AI in robotics enables:

- **Perception:**
  Robots can understand their environment through vision, sound, and other sensory inputs.

- **Decision-Making:**
  Using ML models, robots can choose the best action from a set of possibilities.

- **Learning:**
  Through reinforcement learning, robots can improve their performance based on feedback.

Actionable Tips:

- Start with supervised learning techniques to recognize objects or patterns.

- Experiment with reinforcement learning for tasks like navigation or manipulation.

- Use pre-trained models as a baseline before fine-tuning them for your specific application.

4.2 Step-by-Step: Integrating Machine Learning

1. **Data Collection:**

   o Gather sensor data or images that the robot will use to learn.

2. **Preprocessing:**

   o Clean and normalize the data to ensure consistency.

3. **Model Selection:**

   o Choose an appropriate model (e.g., convolutional neural networks for vision tasks).

4. **Training:**

   o Train your model using available datasets or simulated data.

5. **Integration:**

   o Embed the trained model into your robot's control system to make real-time decisions.

6. **Testing and Refinement:**

- o Validate the model's performance and adjust parameters as needed.

Rhetorical Question:
Imagine a robot that learns to recognize obstacles and adjust its path on its own—each mistake a stepping stone toward perfection. With AI, that vision is within reach.

5. Advanced Sensor Fusion

Modern robots rely on multiple sensors to perceive their environment accurately. Sensor fusion combines data from various sources (like cameras, LIDAR, and IMUs) to create a more complete and reliable picture.

5.1 Why Sensor Fusion?

Each sensor has its strengths and weaknesses. For instance:

- **LIDAR** offers accurate distance measurements but can struggle in poor weather.

- **Cameras** provide rich visual detail but may have issues in low light.

- **IMUs (Inertial Measurement Units)** track movement but can drift over time.

By fusing data from multiple sensors, you can compensate for these limitations and enhance the robot's overall perception.

5.2 Step-by-Step: Implementing Sensor Fusion

1. **Gather Sensor Data:**

   o Collect data from all relevant sensors.

2. **Synchronize Data:**

   o Align the sensor readings in time.

3. **Choose a Fusion Algorithm:**

   o Common approaches include Kalman Filters or Particle Filters.

4. **Combine Data:**

   o Use the selected algorithm to integrate the data into a unified estimate.

5. **Validate the Fusion:**

   o Compare the fused data against known benchmarks or ground truth data.

6. **Refine Parameters:**

   o Adjust the algorithm's parameters to improve accuracy.

Rhetorical Question:
Can you imagine the clarity of vision a robot gains when it combines the strengths of multiple sensors into one cohesive picture? That's the transformative power of sensor fusion.

6. Human–Robot Interaction (HRI) and Collaborative Robotics

Robots are no longer isolated machines—they're increasingly becoming partners in our daily lives. Advanced robotics concepts now include human–robot interaction (HRI) and collaborative robotics, where machines and humans work together seamlessly.

6.1 The Importance of HRI

HRI is about making robots intuitive and user-friendly. It involves:

- **Natural Language Processing (NLP):**
  Allowing robots to understand and respond to voice commands.

- **Gesture Recognition:**
  Interpreting human body language to guide robot behavior.

- **Touch Interfaces and Haptic Feedback:**
  Enabling direct physical interaction.

6.2 Step-by-Step: Implementing HRI

1. **Define Interaction Modalities:**

   o Determine how users will interact with your robot (voice, gesture, touchscreen).

2. **Select Appropriate Sensors:**

   o Use microphones for voice recognition, cameras for gesture detection, and touch sensors for physical interaction.

3. **Implement NLP Algorithms:**

   o Leverage libraries like NLTK or spaCy to process and interpret human language.

4. **Develop a Response Framework:**

   o Create a system where the robot can take appropriate actions based on human inputs.

5. **Test and Refine:**

   o Conduct user tests to ensure that interactions feel natural and intuitive.

6. **Integrate Safety Features:**

   o Ensure that the robot can detect and respond to potential hazards in a human-centric environment.

Rhetorical Question:
Wouldn't it be incredible to work alongside a robot that understands you as naturally as a human partner? Advanced HRI transforms robotic assistance into a collaborative experience.

7. Advanced Simulation and Digital Twin Concepts

Before deploying advanced robotics in the real world, simulation and digital twin technologies allow you to create a virtual replica of your physical system. This not only aids in testing and optimization but also provides valuable insights into long-term performance.

7.1 What is a Digital Twin?

A digital twin is a virtual model of a physical system that mirrors its real-time behavior. Think of it as a high-fidelity simulation that continuously receives data from its physical counterpart, allowing you to predict failures, optimize performance, and plan maintenance.

Key Benefits:

- **Predictive Maintenance:**
  Identify potential issues before they occur.

- **Optimization:**
  Test different scenarios virtually to find the most efficient configuration.

- **Remote Monitoring:**
  Keep track of system performance in real time.

7.2 Step-by-Step: Creating a Digital Twin

1. **Model the Physical System:**

- o Develop a detailed simulation of your robot using tools like Gazebo.

2. **Integrate Real-Time Data:**

   - o Connect your physical robot's sensor data to the digital model.

3. **Implement Feedback Loops:**

   - o Use the digital twin to simulate responses and feed adjustments back to the physical system.

4. **Validate the Model:**

   - o Continuously compare the digital twin's predictions with actual performance.

5. **Optimize Based on Insights:**

   - o Use simulation results to refine your robot's design and control algorithms.

Rhetorical Question:
Imagine being able to test every possible scenario on a virtual replica of your robot before even flipping a switch on the real machine—this is the transformative power of digital twins.

8. Putting It All Together: A Case Study in Advanced Robotics

To bring all these advanced concepts together, let's walk through a comprehensive case study. Imagine you are developing an autonomous delivery robot for an urban environment—a system that requires advanced navigation, robust control, multi-robot coordination, sensor fusion, AI decision-making, and seamless human interaction.

8.1 Defining the Mission

Objective:
Develop an autonomous delivery robot that navigates crowded city streets, avoids obstacles, interacts with pedestrians, and coordinates with other delivery robots for efficient routing.

Key Requirements:

- **Advanced Navigation:**
  Implement SLAM to map the urban environment and determine the robot's location.

- **Robust Control:**
  Use PID and MPC algorithms to maintain stability on uneven terrain.

- **Multi-Robot Coordination:**
  Enable communication among a fleet of robots to optimize delivery routes.

- **Sensor Fusion:**
  Integrate data from LIDAR, cameras, and GPS for reliable perception.

- **AI Integration:**
  Use machine learning to recognize pedestrian gestures and respond to voice commands.

- **Human–Robot Interaction:**
  Develop interfaces that allow customers to track their deliveries and interact with the robot.

8.2 Step-by-Step Implementation

1. **Environment Mapping:**

   o Deploy a SLAM algorithm to create a dynamic map of the delivery area.

2. **Control System Tuning:**

   o Develop and tune PID controllers to manage motor outputs.

3. **Fleet Communication:**

   o Implement a distributed network using ROS2 topics and services for inter-robot communication.

4. **Sensor Integration:**

   o Fuse data from LIDAR, camera, and GPS using a Kalman Filter.

5. **AI-Based Decision Making:**

o Train a neural network to interpret pedestrian gestures.

6. **User Interaction Interface:**

   o Build a mobile app interface for tracking deliveries and sending commands.

7. **Simulation and Testing:**

   o Run extensive simulations using Gazebo and digital twin models to validate performance.

8. **Deployment and Iteration:**

   o Gradually deploy the robots in a controlled urban environment, monitor performance, and iterate.

Actionable Insights:

- **Iterative Development:**
  Break the project into manageable modules and test each rigorously.

- **Data-Driven Optimization:**
  Use simulation data to refine algorithms continuously.

- **User-Centered Design:**
  Engage with potential users early in the design process to tailor HRI elements.

8.3 Case Study System Architecture

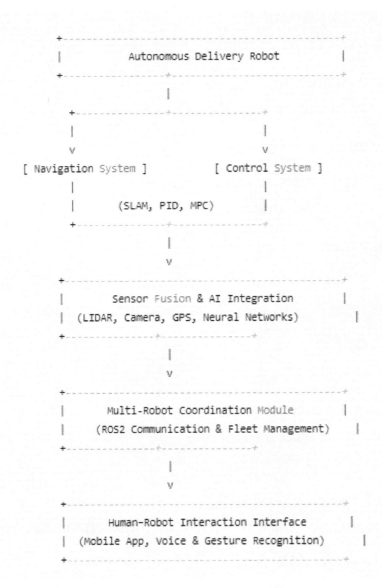

This diagram outlines the integrated system architecture for an autonomous delivery robot, combining all advanced robotics concepts discussed.

Rhetorical Question:
Can you envision a future where fleets of intelligent robots

work together to revolutionize urban logistics? With these advanced robotics concepts, that future is closer than ever.

---

9. Conclusion: The Future of Advanced Robotics

Advanced robotics is not a destination—it's a continuous journey of innovation, learning, and adaptation. By mastering advanced navigation, robust control, multi-robot coordination, sensor fusion, AI integration, and HRI, you're not just building smarter machines—you're shaping the future of technology.

9.1 Recap of Advanced Robotics Concepts

- **Navigation and SLAM:**
  Empowering robots to understand and navigate complex environments.

- **Control Algorithms:**
  Using advanced techniques like PID, MPC, and robust control to ensure precise movement.

- **Multi-Robot Systems:**
  Enabling coordinated action among fleets of robots to enhance efficiency.

- **Artificial Intelligence and Machine Learning:**
  Infusing robots with the ability to learn, adapt, and make intelligent decisions.

- **Sensor Fusion:**
  Combining data from multiple sensors to create a reliable, holistic view of the environment.

- **Human–Robot Interaction:**
  Bridging the gap between humans and machines for collaborative, intuitive operation.

- **Digital Twins and Simulation:**
  Leveraging virtual models to optimize performance and predict outcomes in real time.

9.2 Your Journey Forward

As you continue your journey into advanced robotics, remember that every breakthrough begins with a solid understanding of these fundamental concepts. Whether you're developing next-generation autonomous systems, exploring innovative applications in healthcare, or revolutionizing manufacturing with collaborative robots, the tools and techniques you've learned here will serve as your stepping stones to success.

Rhetorical Question:
Are you ready to lead the charge in creating intelligent, adaptable, and transformative robotic systems? The future of robotics is in your hands, and the possibilities are as limitless as your imagination.

Final Words of Encouragement

Advanced robotics is where art meets science—where creativity fuels technology to solve the most intricate challenges. Embrace every obstacle as an opportunity to innovate, and let your passion for robotics drive you to explore uncharted territories. With every algorithm refined, every sensor fused, and every robot coordinated, you're not just programming a machine—you're crafting the future.

So, gear up, dive deep, and let your journey into advanced robotics transform the way you see technology. The next big breakthrough in robotics could be yours!

Chapter 7: Creating Intelligent and Interactive Systems

Welcome to a deep dive into the art and science of creating intelligent and interactive systems. In today's fast-evolving technological landscape, the fusion of intelligence and interactivity is revolutionizing how machines understand, learn, and respond to their environments and users. In this chapter, we will explore how to design systems that are not only smart—capable of processing data, making decisions, and learning—but also interactive, enabling natural, intuitive communication with humans. Whether you're developing advanced robotics, smart home devices, or next-generation user interfaces, these concepts will empower you to create solutions that adapt and respond to real-world challenges.

In the following sections, we'll break down each concept in clear, jargon-free language, using relatable analogies, step-by-step instructions, and detailed diagrams to illustrate complex ideas. Let's embark on this journey where technology meets human touch, and every system you build becomes a seamless extension of intelligent interaction.

1. Understanding Intelligent and Interactive Systems

Imagine a personal assistant who not only remembers your schedule but also understands your mood and adjusts plans accordingly. Now, envision a robot that can both navigate a room autonomously and hold a conversation with you—these are examples of intelligent and interactive systems at work. But what do these terms really mean?

1.1 Defining Intelligence in Systems

Intelligence in systems refers to the ability of a machine to:

- **Learn:** Adapt from experience by processing data and improving over time.

- **Decide:** Analyze situations and select appropriate actions using algorithms.

- **Perceive:** Interpret sensory input (visual, auditory, tactile) to understand its environment.

Real-World Analogy:
Think of your smartphone. It learns your usage patterns, suggests apps or routes based on your history, and even adjusts settings based on where you are. In robotics, intelligence could mean a robot that recognizes obstacles and plans an optimal path, or a device that personalizes its responses to your voice commands.

1.2 What Makes a System Interactive?

An **interactive** system is one that can engage in a two-way communication process with its users. This means it can:

- **Receive Input:** Understand commands or gestures from a human user.

- **Respond Appropriately:** Provide feedback, perform actions, or communicate results.

- **Adapt Over Time:** Refine its responses based on user behavior and context.

Real-World Analogy:
Consider a conversation with a well-trained customer service agent who not only listens to your questions but also tailors their responses to suit your needs. Interactive systems in technology aim to create that kind of dynamic, responsive communication between humans and machines.

1.3 Why Build Intelligent and Interactive Systems?

The fusion of intelligence and interactivity in systems has several significant advantages:

- **Enhanced User Experience:**
  Systems that understand and respond to user needs create a seamless, engaging experience.

- **Efficiency and Autonomy:**
  Intelligent systems can make decisions on the fly,
  reducing the need for constant human intervention.

- **Scalability:**
  As systems learn and improve, they can adapt to
  increasing complexity and diverse scenarios.

- **Real-World Impact:**
  From autonomous vehicles to smart healthcare
  devices, these systems have the potential to transform
  industries and improve quality of life.

Rhetorical Question:
Imagine if every device you interacted with could learn your
preferences and adjust itself to serve you better—wouldn't
that make your daily life more efficient and enjoyable?
That's the promise of intelligent and interactive systems.

---

2. Designing Intelligent Systems

Designing intelligent systems involves integrating various
technologies and algorithms to enable machines to learn,
decide, and adapt. In this section, we'll explore the key
components and steps necessary to build a system that
possesses genuine intelligence.

2.1 Identifying the Core Functions

Before building an intelligent system, define what "intelligence" means for your specific application. Ask yourself:

- **What decisions should the system make autonomously?**

- **What kind of learning is required (e.g., pattern recognition, predictive analytics)?**

- **What data sources will the system use to learn and adapt?**

Actionable Steps:

1. **Define Objectives:**

   o List the tasks your system should perform autonomously.

   o Example: "The system should predict user preferences based on past interactions."

2. **Determine Data Requirements:**

   o Identify the types of data (sensor readings, user inputs, environmental data) needed to support decision-making.

   o Example: "Collect historical user interaction data, real-time sensor inputs, and contextual information."

3. **Select Learning Methods:**

- o Choose between supervised, unsupervised, or reinforcement learning based on your objectives.

- o Example: "For pattern recognition in user behavior, use supervised learning with labeled datasets."

2.2 Building the Learning Architecture

An intelligent system's architecture typically includes the following components:

- **Data Collection Module:**
  Gathers and preprocesses data from various sources.

- **Learning Module:**
  Implements machine learning algorithms to analyze data and extract insights.

- **Decision Module:**
  Uses learned models to make real-time decisions.

- **Feedback Loop:**
  Continuously refines the system by incorporating new data and outcomes.

Step-by-Step Approach:

1. **Data Collection:**

   - o **Action:** Implement sensors or interfaces to collect relevant data.

   - o **Tip:** Use robust data preprocessing techniques to clean and normalize data.

2. **Model Training:**

   o **Action:** Train your machine learning model on historical or simulated data.

   o **Tip:** Start with a simple model and iterate to more complex architectures as needed.

3. **Decision-Making Integration:**

   o **Action:** Embed the trained model into a real-time control system.

   o **Tip:** Use APIs or frameworks that support fast inference (e.g., TensorFlow Lite for mobile applications).

4. **Feedback Loop:**

   o **Action:** Continuously monitor system performance and update the model with new data.

   o **Tip:** Implement A/B testing to compare different model versions.

2.3 Real-World Example: Intelligent Energy Management System

Imagine an intelligent energy management system in a smart building. This system collects data from temperature sensors, occupancy sensors, and weather forecasts to optimize energy consumption. It learns user preferences, predicts optimal temperature settings, and adjusts heating/cooling in real time to reduce energy waste.

Actionable Steps:

1. **Define Objectives:**

   o Reduce energy consumption by 20% while maintaining comfort.

2. **Data Collection:**

   o Install sensors for temperature, humidity, and occupancy.

   o Integrate weather forecast APIs.

3. **Model Training:**

   o Use historical energy consumption data to train a regression model predicting energy needs.

4. **Decision-Making:**

   o Implement a control system that adjusts HVAC settings based on model predictions.

5. **Feedback Loop:**

   o Continuously monitor energy usage and adjust the model with new data.

Rhetorical Question:
Wouldn't it be remarkable if your building could learn and adjust its energy consumption autonomously, saving money

and reducing environmental impact? That's the power of an intelligently designed system.

---

3. Designing Interactive Systems

An interactive system is all about creating a smooth, engaging dialogue between humans and machines. These systems must be responsive, intuitive, and adaptable, ensuring that the user feels understood and supported.

3.1 Understanding User Interaction

Begin by defining what "interaction" means in the context of your system:

- **Input Methods:**
  How will users communicate with your system? Consider voice, touch, gesture, and even facial expressions.

- **Output Modalities:**
  How will the system respond? Options include visual displays, auditory feedback, haptic feedback, or even physical movements.

- **Context Awareness:**
  How does the system tailor its responses based on the user's context, such as location, time, or emotional state?

Actionable Steps:

1. **Identify User Needs:**

   o Conduct surveys or interviews to understand how users expect to interact with the system.

2. **Map Interaction Scenarios:**

   o Create user journey maps that detail typical interactions.

3. **Define Success Metrics:**

   o Establish criteria such as response time, accuracy of recognition, and user satisfaction ratings.

3.2 Building the Interaction Interface

To create a truly interactive system, you need to design both the hardware (if applicable) and software components of the interface.

Step-by-Step Approach:

1. **Choose the Right Input Devices:**

   o **Voice Recognition:**
   Use microphones and natural language processing (NLP) libraries.

   o **Touch Interfaces:**
   Develop intuitive UI/UX designs for tablets or touchscreens.

- ○ **Gesture Recognition:**
  Incorporate cameras and computer vision algorithms to interpret body language.

2. **Design the Output Channels:**

- ○ **Visual Feedback:**
  Create graphical user interfaces (GUIs) or use augmented reality (AR) displays.

- ○ **Auditory Feedback:**
  Integrate text-to-speech (TTS) systems.

- ○ **Haptic Feedback:**
  Use vibration motors or other tactile devices for physical responses.

3. **Integrate Context Awareness:**

- ○ **Action:** Use sensors (e.g., location trackers, mood detectors) to gather contextual data.

- ○ **Tip:** Implement machine learning models to interpret context and adjust responses accordingly.

3.3 Real-World Example: Interactive Customer Service Robot

Consider an interactive customer service robot deployed in a shopping mall. This robot greets visitors, answers questions about store locations, and even provides personalized recommendations based on user interactions.

Actionable Steps:

1. **Define the Interaction Scope:**

   o Determine the primary functions: greeting, information retrieval, and personalized recommendations.

2. **Select Input Devices:**

   o Integrate a microphone for voice commands and a touchscreen for visual queries.

3. **Implement Processing Algorithms:**

   o Use NLP libraries such as spaCy or NLTK to interpret customer queries.

4. **Develop a Response Framework:**

   o Create a dialogue management system that matches inputs with appropriate responses.

5. **Test with Real Users:**

   o Run pilot tests in the mall and gather feedback to refine the interaction experience.

Rhetorical Question:
Wouldn't it be delightful to interact with a robot that not only understands your questions but also responds in a friendly, conversational manner—almost like chatting with a helpful friend? That's the essence of an interactive system.

4. Step-by-Step Guide to Building a Prototype

Now that we've explored the theoretical aspects of creating intelligent and interactive systems, it's time to roll up our sleeves and build a prototype. This hands-on guide will walk you through creating a simple yet robust system that can understand user commands and respond intelligently.

4.1 Planning Your Prototype

Actionable Steps:

1. **Define the Purpose:**

   o **Example:** "Build a smart assistant that can answer basic queries about the weather and time."

2. **List Required Components:**

   o **Input:** Voice recognition using a microphone.

   o **Processing:** Natural language processing (NLP) to interpret commands.

   o **Output:** Text-to-speech (TTS) for verbal responses and a simple GUI for visual feedback.

3. **Sketch a Workflow:**

   o Draw a flowchart that maps out how user input is captured, processed, and responded to.

4.2 Setting Up the Development Environment

Before coding, ensure you have the necessary tools:

- **Python Environment:** Use a virtual environment to manage dependencies.

- **Libraries:** Install essential libraries such as speech_recognition, pyttsx3 (for TTS), and flask or tkinter (for GUI).

Step-by-Step:

1. **Create and Activate a Virtual Environment:**

bash

python -m venv smart_assistant_env

source smart_assistant_env/bin/activate

2. **Install Libraries:**

bash

pip install SpeechRecognition pyttsx3 tkinter

3. **Set Up Version Control:**

   o Initialize a Git repository for version tracking.

4.3 Writing the Code

Let's break down the code into manageable modules:

Module 1: Voice Input Module

```python

import speech_recognition as sr

def capture_voice():
    recognizer = sr.Recognizer()
    with sr.Microphone() as source:
        print("Listening...")
        audio = recognizer.listen(source)
    try:
        command =
recognizer.recognize_google(audio)
        print("You said:", command)
        return command
    except sr.UnknownValueError:
        print("Sorry, I did not understand
that.")
        return None
    except sr.RequestError:
        print("Could not request results; check
your network.")
        return None
```

Module 2: Natural Language Processing Module

python

```python
def interpret_command(command):
    if command:
        command = command.lower()
        if "weather" in command:
            return "The weather today is sunny
with a high of 25°C."
        elif "time" in command:
            from datetime import datetime
            return f"The current time is
{datetime.now().strftime('%H:%M:%S')}."
    return "I'm not sure how to help with that."
```

Module 3: Text-to-Speech Output Module

python

```python
import pyttsx3

def speak_response(response):
    engine = pyttsx3.init()
    engine.say(response)
    engine.runAndWait()
```

Module 4: Integrating with a Simple GUI (Optional)

Using Tkinter for a basic GUI:

python

```python
import tkinter as tk

def create_gui(response):
    window = tk.Tk()
    window.title("Smart Assistant")
    label = tk.Label(window, text=response,
font=("Arial", 14))
    label.pack(padx=20, pady=20)
    window.mainloop()
```

Module 5: Main Integration Script

python

```python
def main():
    command = capture_voice()
    response = interpret_command(command)
    print("Response:", response)
    speak_response(response)
    create_gui(response)


if __name__ == "__main__":
    main()
```

Rhetorical Question:

Wouldn't it be empowering to see your code come alive as a smart assistant that listens, interprets, and speaks back to you? This is the essence of building interactive systems.

4.4 Testing and Iteration

Actionable Steps:

1. **Run the Prototype:**

    o Execute your main script and test various voice commands.

2. **Gather Feedback:**

    o Observe how the system responds and note any inaccuracies or delays.

3. **Refine Modules:**

    o Tweak parameters in the voice recognition and NLP modules.

    o Optimize TTS output for clarity and natural speech.

4. **Iterate:**

    o Continuously test and improve the system, adding new commands and functionalities.

---

5. Enhancing Intelligence with Advanced Features

Now that you have a basic prototype, it's time to add advanced features to make your system truly intelligent and interactive.

5.1 Integrating Context Awareness

Context awareness allows your system to tailor its responses based on the situation. For example, a smart assistant could respond differently when you're at home versus in a car.

Actionable Steps:

1. **Collect Context Data:**

   o Use sensors or APIs (e.g., location services, calendar events).

2. **Implement Conditional Logic:**

   o Adjust responses based on context.

   o Example: "If at home, suggest turning on the lights; if in the car, provide navigation assistance."

3. **Test Contextual Responses:**

   o Simulate different contexts and verify that the system adapts accordingly.

5.2 Adding Machine Learning Capabilities

To further enhance intelligence, consider integrating machine learning (ML) models to analyze patterns and improve decision-making.

Step-by-Step:

1. **Data Collection:**

   o Record user interactions and system responses.

2. **Model Training:**

   o Use collected data to train a model (e.g., sentiment analysis for voice commands).

3. **Integration:**

   o Deploy the trained model into your system for real-time predictions.

4. **Continuous Learning:**

   o Implement mechanisms to update the model with new data over time.

5.3 Improving User Interaction Through Personalization

Personalization tailors the system's responses to individual users, increasing satisfaction and engagement.

Actionable Steps:

1. **User Profiling:**

   o Collect preferences, interaction history, and feedback.

2. **Adaptive Response Mechanisms:**

   o Adjust responses based on the user profile.

3. **Iterative Testing:**

   o Continuously refine personalization algorithms based on user feedback.

Rhetorical Question:

Wouldn't it be remarkable if your system could learn your unique preferences and adjust its behavior just for you—almost like a personal concierge? Personalization is key to achieving that level of interaction.

---

6. Implementing Natural Language Understanding (NLU)

A cornerstone of interactive systems is the ability to understand natural language. Natural Language Understanding (NLU) involves parsing user inputs, identifying intents, and extracting relevant information.

6.1 Basics of NLU

NLU can transform raw voice or text input into actionable commands. It involves:

- **Intent Recognition:**
  Determining what the user wants (e.g., "What's the weather today?").

- **Entity Extraction:**
  Identifying key details (e.g., location, date, time).

Actionable Steps:

1. **Select an NLU Library:**

   o Libraries such as spaCy, Rasa, or NLTK offer robust tools for NLU.

2. **Train a Simple Model:**

   o   Use labeled data to train your system on common commands.

3. **Integrate with Your Prototype:**

   o   Replace simple keyword matching with the trained NLU model for more accurate interpretation.

4. **Test with Diverse Inputs:**

   o   Validate the model against various accents, dialects, and phrasing.

Rhetorical Question:
Imagine conversing with a system that understands not just your words, but the meaning behind them—transforming casual conversation into precise, actionable tasks. That's the promise of robust NLU.

---

7. Enhancing System Responsiveness with Real-Time Feedback

For an interactive system to feel truly alive, it must provide immediate, contextually appropriate feedback. Real-time responsiveness bridges the gap between user intent and system action.

7.1 Techniques for Real-Time Processing

- **Asynchronous Programming:**
  Use asynchronous frameworks to handle multiple tasks simultaneously without blocking.

- **Optimized Data Pipelines:**
  Ensure that data flows swiftly from input to processing and output.

- **Efficient Hardware Utilization:**
  Leverage multi-core processors and, where applicable, GPU acceleration for intensive tasks.

Step-by-Step Approach:

1. **Implement Asynchronous Functions:**

   - Use Python's asyncio library to process inputs and generate outputs concurrently.

2. **Optimize Algorithms:**

   - Profile your code to identify bottlenecks and optimize critical sections.

3. **Monitor System Latency:**

   - Use logging and monitoring tools to track response times and adjust configurations.

7.2 Real-Time Feedback Loop

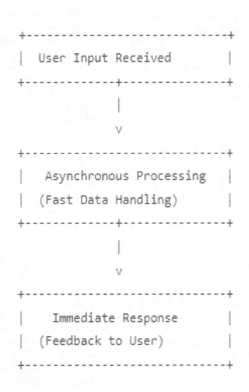

```
+-----------------------------+
|  User Input Received        |
+--------------+--------------+
               |
               v
+-----------------------------+
|   Asynchronous Processing   |
|   (Fast Data Handling)      |
+--------------+--------------+
               |
               v
+-----------------------------+
|    Immediate Response       |
|   (Feedback to User)        |
+-----------------------------+
```

This diagram illustrates the flow of real-time processing from capturing user input to delivering immediate feedback.

Rhetorical Question:
Wouldn't it be frustrating to interact with a system that lags or delays responses? Real-time feedback ensures a smooth, engaging, and natural interaction experience.

8. Testing, Evaluating, and Iterating on Your System

No intelligent and interactive system is complete without rigorous testing and continuous improvement. Iterative development ensures that your system evolves based on real-world usage and feedback.

8.1 Creating a Testing Framework

Actionable Steps:

1. **Define Test Cases:**

   o Identify key functionalities such as voice recognition accuracy, response time, and user satisfaction.

2. **Automate Testing:**

   o Develop scripts that simulate user interactions and record system responses.

3. **Collect Metrics:**

   o Track performance indicators (e.g., latency, error rates, user engagement) to evaluate system performance.

9. Real-World Case Study: An Intelligent Interactive Kiosk

To illustrate the integration of advanced concepts, let's consider a real-world case study: developing an intelligent interactive kiosk for a museum.

9.1 Project Overview

Objective:
Create a kiosk that provides visitors with personalized tours, answers questions about exhibits, and adapts to user preferences in real time.

Key Features:

- **Voice and Touch Input:**
  Allows visitors to ask questions or select options.

- **Contextual Awareness:**
  Uses location data within the museum to provide relevant information.

- **Personalized Responses:**
  Remembers visitor preferences and adapts its responses.

- **Visual and Auditory Feedback:**
  Combines on-screen information with audio narration.

9.2 Implementation Steps

1. **Design the User Interface:**

- o Develop a clean, intuitive GUI for touchscreen interaction.

- o Integrate voice recognition to accept spoken queries.

2. **Integrate Intelligent Features:**

- o Use NLP to interpret questions.

- o Employ machine learning to analyze visitor behavior and personalize responses.

3. **Deploy Context Awareness:**

- o Use indoor positioning systems to detect the visitor's location.

- o Provide tailored content based on exhibit proximity.

4. **Implement a Feedback Loop:**

- o Collect usage data to refine recommendations and interface design over time.

Intelligent Interactive Kiosk Architecture

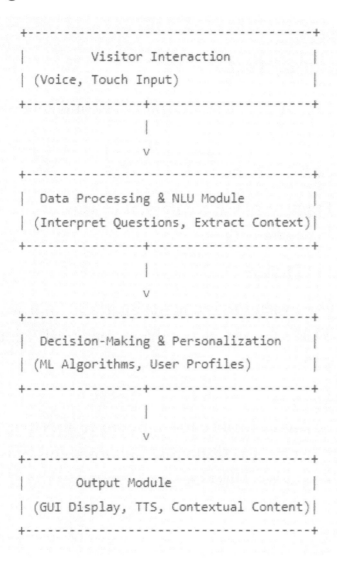

This diagram summarizes the architectural components of an intelligent interactive kiosk, emphasizing the integration of user input, data processing, decision-making, and output.

9.3 Evaluating the System

Actionable Steps:

1. **Conduct User Trials:**

   o Deploy the kiosk in a pilot area and collect user feedback.

2. **Measure Key Metrics:**

   o Track response accuracy, user satisfaction, and engagement time.

3. **Iterate on Design:**

   o Use insights to refine the interface, improve NLU accuracy, and enhance personalization features.

Rhetorical Question:
Wouldn't it be transformative for museum visitors to interact with a system that feels as responsive and insightful as a knowledgeable guide? This case study embodies the potential of intelligent and interactive systems to enrich real-world experiences.

10. Best Practices and Future Directions

Creating intelligent and interactive systems is an evolving field. As you continue to innovate, keep these best practices in mind:

10.1 Best Practices

- **User-Centered Design:**
    - Involve end-users early in the development process.
    - Continuously gather and act on feedback.

- **Modular Development:**
    - Build your system in independent, testable modules.
    - This facilitates debugging and future enhancements.

- **Continuous Learning:**
    - Implement feedback loops not only in the system's functionality but also in your development process.
    - Stay updated with the latest research and technology trends.

- **Scalability:**

- Design your system so it can be scaled up (more users, more data) without a complete overhaul.

- **Robust Testing:**

  - Use both simulated and real-world testing to validate system performance.

10.2 Future Directions

As technology evolves, so will the capabilities of intelligent and interactive systems. Here are some trends to watch:

- **Integration of Augmented Reality (AR):**

  - Combine physical and digital worlds to create immersive interactions.

- **Edge Computing:**

  - Process data locally for faster, real-time decision-making.

- **Advanced AI Models:**

  - Leverage state-of-the-art deep learning techniques to further improve system intelligence.

- **Increased Interconnectivity:**

  - Develop systems that can seamlessly interact with other devices and networks, creating truly smart environments.

Rhetorical Question:

Imagine a world where every device, from your refrigerator to your car, communicates intelligently with you and with each other. How would that transform your daily life? The future of intelligent and interactive systems is bright and boundless.

11. Conclusion: Shaping the Future Through Intelligent Interaction

In this chapter, we have journeyed through the process of creating intelligent and interactive systems—from understanding their fundamental principles to designing, prototyping, and enhancing them with advanced features. You now have a comprehensive roadmap to build systems that not only make smart decisions but also engage with users in a natural and intuitive manner.

Recap of Key Learnings

- **Core Concepts:**
  We defined what it means for a system to be intelligent and interactive, focusing on learning, decision-making, and natural human-machine communication.

- **Design Principles:**
  We explored the essential components and architectures necessary to build these systems,

including data collection, learning modules, decision-making frameworks, and feedback loops.

- **Implementation Strategies:**
  Through practical, step-by-step guides, we demonstrated how to create prototypes—from simple voice-activated assistants to complex interactive kiosks.

- **Advanced Enhancements:**
  We delved into techniques like context awareness, machine learning integration, and natural language understanding to elevate system performance.

- **Evaluation and Iteration:**
  Emphasizing the importance of testing, user feedback, and continuous improvement, we set the stage for building systems that evolve and improve over time.

- **Real-World Impact:**
  Through case studies and best practices, we highlighted how these systems are already transforming industries—from autonomous delivery robots to personalized customer service.

Your Path Forward

As you move forward in your journey to create intelligent and interactive systems, keep in mind that the process is iterative. Every prototype is an opportunity to learn, refine, and innovate. Here are your next steps:

1. **Experiment and Innovate:**

- o Apply the concepts discussed to your own projects.

- o Don't be afraid to push boundaries and try new approaches.

2. **Collaborate and Share:**

   - o Engage with the vibrant community of developers, researchers, and enthusiasts.

   - o Share your projects, gather feedback, and contribute to the collective knowledge.

3. **Stay Curious:**

   - o The field of intelligent and interactive systems is rapidly evolving.

   - o Continuously educate yourself on new technologies, tools, and methodologies.

4. **Build for Impact:**

   - o Focus on real-world applications that can improve efficiency, enhance user experiences, and solve pressing challenges.

   - o Whether you're developing for healthcare, smart cities, education, or entertainment, your work can make a meaningful difference.

Rhetorical Question:

Are you ready to build the next generation of systems that not only think but also connect with people on a personal level? The tools and techniques you've learned in this chapter are your stepping stones to creating technologies that will shape the future.

12. Final Reflective Thought

Creating intelligent and interactive systems is about more than just technology—it's about bridging the gap between human intuition and machine precision. Every system you design has the potential to revolutionize how we interact with the digital world, making it more responsive, empathetic, and adaptive to our needs.

Take a moment to reflect on the possibilities:

- Envision a world where every device understands your preferences and anticipates your needs.

- Picture robots that can not only perform tasks but also engage in meaningful conversations.

- Imagine systems that continuously learn from you, growing smarter and more intuitive over time.

With passion, creativity, and a relentless drive to innovate, you have the power to make that vision a reality.

13. Resources for Continued Learning

To help you on your journey, here are some resources and tools that can further deepen your knowledge and expand your skills:

- **Online Courses and Tutorials:**
  - Coursera, Udemy, and edX offer courses on artificial intelligence, machine learning, and human-robot interaction.

- **Books:**
  - "Artificial Intelligence: A Modern Approach" by Stuart Russell and Peter Norvig.
  - "Designing Bots" by Amir Shevat.

- **Communities and Forums:**
  - GitHub repositories for open-source projects.
  - ROS Discourse and Stack Overflow for robotics-specific queries.
  - Meetup groups and conferences on AI, robotics, and interactive systems.

- **Tools and Libraries:**
  - Python libraries: TensorFlow, PyTorch, spaCy, and NLTK.
  - Simulation platforms: Gazebo, RViz, and Webots.

   o   NLU frameworks: Rasa, Dialogflow, and Microsoft LUIS.

Rhetorical Question:
Wouldn't it be amazing to have a toolbox full of resources at your fingertips, ready to help you overcome any challenge in building intelligent and interactive systems? Keep exploring, keep learning, and never stop innovating.

---

14. Final Words

As we conclude this chapter on creating intelligent and interactive systems, remember that the future is yours to shape. The ideas, tools, and methodologies discussed here are only the beginning. With every project, every line of code, and every interaction you design, you are contributing to a future where technology becomes a natural, seamless extension of human capability.

Embrace the challenges, celebrate your breakthroughs, and continue to push the boundaries of what's possible. Your journey into intelligent and interactive systems is not just about building smarter machines—it's about creating a world where technology and humanity thrive together.

Happy building, and here's to the intelligent, interactive future that you will create!

Chapter 8: Multi-Robot Systems and Collaborative Robotics

Welcome to the frontier of robotics, where teamwork among machines transforms individual capability into collective brilliance. In this chapter, we dive deep into the world of multi-robot systems and collaborative robotics—a domain where robots communicate, coordinate, and work together to achieve goals that would be impossible for a lone machine. Whether you're developing autonomous delivery fleets, search-and-rescue teams, or smart manufacturing lines, this guide will equip you with the insights and techniques to design systems that operate harmoniously in unison.

We'll break down advanced concepts into clear, jargon-free language, using relatable analogies, step-by-step instructions, and visual aids to illustrate every idea. So, let's embark on this journey into collaborative robotics and discover how to turn a group of individual robots into an efficient, synchronized team.

1. Introduction: The Power of Many in Robotics

Imagine trying to move a large, heavy object by yourself. Now imagine working together with a team where each person contributes a small effort, yet the collective power makes the task effortless. That is the essence of multi-robot systems: a group of robots, each with its unique strengths, working collaboratively to achieve a common objective.

1.1 Why Multi-Robot Systems?

Multi-robot systems (MRS) provide numerous benefits:

- **Efficiency and Speed:**
  A fleet of robots can cover more ground and perform tasks faster than a single robot.

- **Redundancy and Reliability:**
  If one robot fails, others can compensate, ensuring the mission continues without interruption.

- **Scalability:**
  Systems can be expanded with additional robots to handle larger tasks or more complex environments.

- **Flexibility:**
  Different robots can specialize in specific tasks, from sensing to manipulation, enabling versatile operations.

Rhetorical Question:
Wouldn't it be amazing if your team of robots could

coordinate seamlessly—each one adapting its role in real time to overcome challenges together?

1.2 Collaborative Robotics: An Overview

Collaborative robotics extends beyond simply having multiple robots in one space; it's about enabling them to interact intelligently. This involves:

- **Inter-Robot Communication:**
  Sharing information such as positions, sensor data, and task status.

- **Task Allocation:**
  Dividing tasks among robots based on their capabilities and current workload.

- **Coordination and Synchronization:**
  Ensuring that actions are well-timed and resources are used efficiently.

Real-World Analogy:
Think of a relay race where each runner must pass the baton smoothly. Similarly, in multi-robot systems, coordination ensures that each robot's output seamlessly becomes the input for the next step.

Multi-Robot Systems Overview

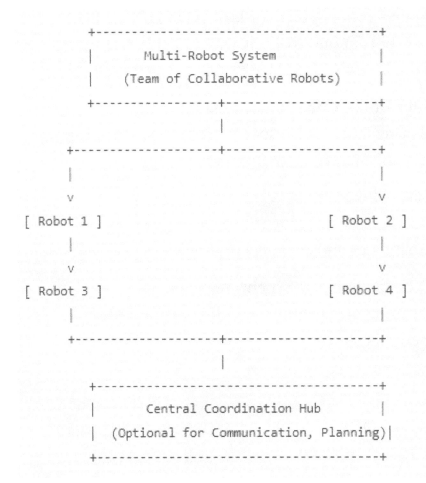

```
        +---------------------------------------+
        |        Multi-Robot System             |
        |    (Team of Collaborative Robots)     |
        +-----------------+---------------------+
                          |
        +-----------------+---------------------+
        |                                       |
        v                                       v
   [ Robot 1 ]                            [ Robot 2 ]
        |                                       |
        v                                       v
   [ Robot 3 ]                            [ Robot 4 ]
        |                                       |
        +-----------------+---------------------+
                          |
        +---------------------------------------+
        |        Central Coordination Hub       |
        |  (Optional for Communication, Planning)|
        +---------------------------------------+
```

This diagram shows multiple robots working together, optionally coordinated by a central hub to ensure synchronization and effective communication.

2. Fundamental Concepts of Multi-Robot Systems

Before designing complex multi-robot systems, it's important to understand the basic building blocks. We'll break down the core concepts that enable robots to work together effectively.

2.1 Nodes and Communication

In a multi-robot system, each robot can be thought of as a "node" in a larger network. These nodes communicate using standardized messages—much like sending emails or texts—to share critical information.

Key Components:

- **Nodes:**
  Individual robots or processes running on them.

- **Topics and Messages:**
  Channels for communication; for instance, a topic might be "robot_status" where each robot posts its current position and state.

- **Services:**
  Request-response interactions for more immediate communication.

- **Actions:**
  For long-duration tasks that can provide continuous feedback.

Step-by-Step: Setting Up Basic Communication

1. **Define Communication Channels:**

   o List the topics required (e.g., location updates, sensor readings, task statuses).

2. **Implement Message Passing:**

   o Use ROS2 (Robot Operating System 2) or another middleware to establish channels.

3. **Test Inter-Robot Communication:**

   o Ensure messages sent by one robot are received by others.

Actionable Tip:
Start with simple status updates and gradually add complexity to the message content as you validate the communication infrastructure.

2.2 Task Allocation and Role Assignment

For robots to work together, they must understand which tasks need to be done and which robot is best suited for each task. This involves both pre-defined roles and dynamic task allocation based on real-time conditions.

Step-by-Step: Task Allocation Process

1. **Identify Tasks:**

   o Break the mission into individual tasks (e.g., mapping, object retrieval, obstacle clearing).

2. **Define Robot Capabilities:**

   o List the strengths and limitations of each robot.

3. **Assign Roles:**

   o Use algorithms or manual planning to allocate tasks to each robot.

4. **Monitor and Reassign:**

   o Continuously monitor performance and reassign tasks if a robot becomes overloaded or encounters issues.

Actionable Tip:
Consider using a centralized planner for small teams and distributed planning for larger swarms, where robots negotiate tasks amongst themselves.

---

3. Communication and Coordination Strategies

Effective collaboration in multi-robot systems relies on robust communication and coordination strategies. Let's explore how robots share information and synchronize their actions to work as one cohesive unit.

3.1 Communication Protocols

Communication protocols ensure that messages between robots are clear, timely, and reliable. Here's how to set up a basic protocol:

Step-by-Step: Establishing a Communication Protocol

1. **Select a Middleware Platform:**

    o Popular options include ROS2, MQTT, and ZeroMQ.

2. **Define Message Formats:**

    o Standardize the structure of messages (e.g., JSON, XML, or custom formats).

3. **Implement Reliable Delivery:**

    o Use acknowledgment mechanisms to ensure messages are received.

4. **Test Under Load:**

    o Simulate high-traffic scenarios to ensure the protocol holds up.

Actionable Tip:
Start with ROS2's built-in messaging system, which provides robust support for multi-robot communication out of the box.

3.2 Coordination Algorithms

Once communication is in place, the next challenge is coordinating actions. Coordination algorithms ensure that robots do not work at cross purposes and that they can efficiently share resources and information.

Common Coordination Strategies:

- **Centralized Coordination:**
  A central controller makes decisions for all robots.
  Pros: Simplifies decision-making;
  Cons: Can become a bottleneck.

- **Decentralized Coordination:**
  Robots make decisions locally and communicate with neighbors.
  Pros: More scalable and robust to failures;
  Cons: More complex to implement.

- **Hybrid Approaches:**
  Combine centralized planning with decentralized execution for flexibility and robustness.

Step-by-Step: Implementing Decentralized Coordination

1. **Establish Local Communication:**

   o Ensure each robot can communicate with its immediate neighbors.

2. **Define Local Decision Rules:**

- o Create simple rules for how a robot should react to its neighbors' actions.

3. **Test with Simulations:**

- o Use simulation environments to validate that local decisions lead to a coherent global behavior.

4. **Refine Based on Feedback:**

- o Adjust the rules and communication range to optimize performance.

Decentralized Coordination Flow

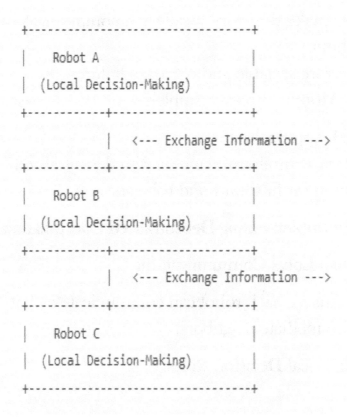

```
+-------------------------------------+
|    Robot A                          |
|  (Local Decision-Making)            |
+-------------+-----------------------+
              |   <--- Exchange Information --->
+-------------+-----------------------+
|    Robot B                          |
|  (Local Decision-Making)            |
+-------------+-----------------------+
              |   <--- Exchange Information --->
+-------------+-----------------------+
|    Robot C                          |
|  (Local Decision-Making)            |
+-------------------------------------+
```

This diagram shows how robots in a decentralized system share information with their neighbors and make local decisions that collectively lead to coordinated behavior.

Rhetorical Question:
Can you imagine a swarm of drones navigating through a disaster zone, each one adjusting its path based on real-time updates from its neighbors? That's the power of decentralized coordination in action.

---

4. Collaborative Robotics: How Robots Work Together

Beyond mere coordination, collaborative robotics involves robots working together on shared tasks, often with specialized roles. This synergy enables more complex operations and efficient problem-solving.

4.1 Defining Collaboration

Collaboration in robotics is about more than just communication; it's about synergy. In a collaborative system, robots:

- **Share Resources:**
  Work together to use sensors, tools, and computational power.

- **Divide and Conquer:**
  Split tasks into manageable sub-tasks that each robot handles.

- **Support Each Other:**
  Provide backup when one robot faces a challenge, ensuring the overall mission stays on track.

Real-World Analogy:
Consider a group of chefs in a busy kitchen. Each chef has a specific role—one handles the grill, another prepares sauces, and another plates the food. Their collaborative effort results in a delicious meal prepared efficiently. In robotics, each robot's specialized function contributes to a successful outcome.

4.2 Step-by-Step: Building a Collaborative System

1. **Identify Shared Goals:**

   o Clearly define the overall mission that requires collaboration.

2. **Break Down the Mission:**

   o Divide the mission into sub-tasks that can be assigned to individual robots.

3. **Develop a Communication Framework:**

   o Establish channels for sharing progress and data.

4. **Implement Support Mechanisms:**

- o Create protocols for how robots can assist each other if one encounters difficulties.

5. **Test in Simulated Environments:**

   - o Validate that the collaborative behavior leads to efficient task completion.

6. **Iterate and Refine:**

   - o Adjust task divisions and support protocols based on performance data.

Rhetorical Question:
Imagine a team of robots working together to assemble a complex structure—each robot playing a specific part, seamlessly handing off tasks. That's the transformative potential of collaborative robotics.

---

5. Step-by-Step Implementation of Multi-Robot Systems

Let's move from theory to practice with a comprehensive, step-by-step guide on implementing a multi-robot system.

5.1 Preparation and Planning

Actionable Steps:

1. **Define the Mission:**

   - o Clearly outline the tasks (e.g., area exploration, object transport).

2. **Determine Robot Roles:**

   o Assign roles based on robot capabilities (e.g., leader, follower, scout).

3. **Select Communication Protocols:**

   o Choose middleware (e.g., ROS2) to facilitate reliable message passing.

4. **Sketch System Architecture:**

   o Draw a high-level diagram that outlines how the robots will interact.

5.2 Setting Up the Hardware and Software Environment

Hardware Setup:

- **Robot Units:**
  Ensure each robot is equipped with the necessary sensors, actuators, and communication modules.

- **Central Controller (Optional):**
  If using a centralized approach, set up a controller to coordinate tasks.

Software Setup:

1. **Install ROS2 on Each Robot:**

   o Follow platform-specific installation guides.

2. **Configure Network Settings:**

o Ensure all robots can communicate over the same network.

3. **Deploy Base Software Packages:**

  o Install and configure packages for navigation, communication, and task management.

Step-by-Step Checklist:

- Define mission and roles.

- Set up hardware for each robot.

- Install and configure ROS2.

- Verify network connectivity between robots.

- Deploy base software modules.

5.3 Writing the Coordination Code

Using a modular approach, write code that enables each robot to:

- **Broadcast Its Status:**
  Regularly publish its position, task status, and sensor data.

- **Receive Commands:**
  Listen for task assignments and coordination messages.

- **Execute Local Decision-Making:**
  Adjust actions based on local sensor data and received information.

Example (Pseudo-Code):

```python
import rclpy
from rclpy.node import Node
from std_msgs.msg import String, Float32

class RobotNode(Node):
    def __init__(self):
        super().__init__('robot_node')
        self.publisher = self.create_publisher(String, 'robot_status', 10)
        self.subscriber = self.create_subscription(String,
        'task_assignment', self.task_callback, 10)
        self.timer = self.create_timer(1.0,
        self.broadcast_status)

    def broadcast_status(self):
        status_msg = String()
        status_msg.data = "Robot A at (x, y)
        performing task..."
        self.publisher.publish(status_msg)
        self.get_logger().info("Broadcasting
        status")

    def task_callback(self, msg):
```

```
        self.get_logger().info("Received task: "
+ msg.data)
        # Implement decision-making logic based
on task assignment
        # For example, update robot state or
reallocate tasks
```

Actionable Tip:

Modularize your code so that each robot's decision-making, communication, and control logic are encapsulated in separate functions. This makes debugging and future enhancements easier.

5.4 Testing and Debugging the System

Testing Steps:

1. **Simulate a Multi-Robot Environment:**

   o Use simulation tools (e.g., Gazebo) to test inter-robot communication and task coordination.

2. **Monitor ROS2 Topics:**

   o Use ros2 topic list and ros2 topic echo to ensure that messages are being sent and received correctly.

3. **Iteratively Debug:**

   o Test individual modules before integrating them into the full system.

   o Use logging to capture key events and errors.

Rhetorical Question:
Can you imagine the confidence of knowing that your fleet of robots is not only communicating effectively but also dynamically adapting to real-time challenges? That's the assurance of a well-tested, coordinated multi-robot system.

---

6. Real-World Applications and Case Studies

Multi-robot systems and collaborative robotics are not just academic concepts—they're actively transforming industries. Let's explore some real-world applications and case studies that illustrate the power of these systems.

6.1 Industrial Automation

In manufacturing, fleets of robots work together to assemble products, manage inventory, and optimize workflows. Collaborative robots (cobots) work alongside human workers, enhancing productivity and safety.

Case Study: Automated Warehouse

- **Objective:**
  Automate the inventory management process in a large warehouse.

- **Implementation:**
  A fleet of robots is deployed to transport goods, scan barcodes, and update inventory databases in real time.

- **Results:**
  Increased efficiency, reduced human error, and faster order fulfillment.

6.2 Search and Rescue

Multi-robot systems are crucial in disaster response scenarios. Drones, ground robots, and aquatic robots work together to search for survivors, map hazardous areas, and deliver aid.

Case Study: Disaster Response Swarm

- **Objective:**
  Deploy a swarm of drones and ground robots to locate survivors after a natural disaster.

- **Implementation:**
  Robots use SLAM to navigate rubble, share sensor data to identify safe paths, and coordinate rescue efforts.

- **Results:**
  Faster search times, improved safety for rescue teams, and more efficient resource allocation.

6.3 Autonomous Delivery Systems

In urban environments, collaborative robotics enable the operation of autonomous delivery fleets. These robots work together to optimize delivery routes, avoid obstacles, and ensure timely delivery.

Case Study: Urban Delivery Fleet

- **Objective:**
  Create a fleet of delivery robots that can navigate crowded city streets.

- **Implementation:**
  Robots communicate via ROS2, share traffic and obstacle data, and dynamically reroute to ensure efficiency.

- **Results:**
  Reduced delivery times, decreased operational costs, and enhanced customer satisfaction.

Rhetorical Question:
Imagine a world where fleets of robots work tirelessly behind the scenes, ensuring your packages arrive on time and industrial processes run smoothly—this is the reality of collaborative robotics today.

---

7. Challenges and Solutions in Multi-Robot Systems

While the benefits of multi-robot systems are immense, they come with their own set of challenges. Understanding these challenges—and knowing how to address them—is critical for building robust systems.

7.1 Common Challenges

- **Communication Overhead:**
  As the number of robots increases, the volume of data exchanged can overwhelm the network.

- **Coordination Complexity:**
  Ensuring that multiple robots do not interfere with each other's tasks can be difficult.

- **Scalability Issues:**
  Algorithms that work for a small team may not scale well for larger fleets.

- **Robustness and Fault Tolerance:**
  The failure of one robot should not derail the entire system.

- **Latency and Real-Time Constraints:**
  Delays in communication or processing can lead to suboptimal performance or even collisions.

7.2 Step-by-Step: Addressing Challenges

1. **Optimize Communication:**

   - **Action:** Use efficient message formats and limit unnecessary data exchange.

   - **Tip:** Employ techniques such as data compression or priority-based messaging.

2. **Implement Decentralized Coordination:**

- o **Action:** Allow robots to make local decisions and reduce dependency on a central controller.

- o **Tip:** Use consensus algorithms to ensure coherent group behavior.

3. **Scalability Testing:**

- o **Action:** Simulate scenarios with increasing numbers of robots.

- o **Tip:** Identify bottlenecks early and adjust protocols or algorithms accordingly.

4. **Enhance Fault Tolerance:**

- o **Action:** Design fallback strategies where robots can compensate for the failure of a peer.

- o **Tip:** Implement watchdog timers and self-diagnostic routines.

5. **Minimize Latency:**

- o **Action:** Optimize code, reduce computational complexity, and consider edge computing.

- o **Tip:** Use profiling tools to detect and eliminate latency issues.

Rhetorical Question:
Wouldn't it be reassuring to know that every potential pitfall in your multi-robot system is anticipated and addressed, ensuring smooth and reliable operation even in complex environments?

8. Future Trends in Collaborative Robotics

The field of collaborative robotics is rapidly evolving, with exciting advancements on the horizon. Staying informed about future trends can help you design systems that are not only effective today but also future-proof.

8.1 Emerging Technologies and Innovations

- **Swarm Robotics:**
  Large numbers of simple robots working together to achieve complex tasks through emergent behavior.

- **Artificial Intelligence Integration:**
  Deep learning models that enhance decision-making, improve perception, and enable more natural interactions.

- **Edge Computing and 5G:**
  Faster data processing and communication, enabling real-time collaboration even in large-scale deployments.

- **Human-Robot Collaboration:**
  Systems that seamlessly integrate human input, using augmented reality (AR) and wearable technologies to enhance collaboration.

- **Cyber-Physical Systems and Digital Twins:**
  Virtual replicas of physical systems that enable predictive maintenance and system optimization.

8.2 Preparing for the Future

Actionable Steps:

1. **Invest in Research and Development:**

   o Keep abreast of the latest academic research, attend conferences, and collaborate with industry experts.

2. **Adopt Flexible Architectures:**

   o Design systems that can incorporate new technologies and algorithms as they become available.

3. **Prototype and Experiment:**

   o Regularly test emerging technologies in controlled environments.

4. **Foster Interdisciplinary Collaboration:**

   o Work with experts in AI, networking, and human factors to create truly integrated solutions.

5. **Plan for Scalability:**

   o Ensure that your systems are designed to scale from small teams to large swarms.

Imagine a future where thousands of robots operate as a cohesive swarm, dynamically adapting to every challenge, and where human and machine collaboration is seamless— aren't you excited to be part of that revolution?

---

9. Conclusion: Building the Future Together

Multi-robot systems and collaborative robotics are more than just a collection of machines working in parallel—they represent a paradigm shift in how we approach automation, problem-solving, and human-machine interaction. In this chapter, we've explored:

- **Fundamental Concepts:**
  Understanding nodes, communication protocols, and task allocation.

- **Coordination and Collaboration:**
  Strategies for decentralized decision-making and collaborative task execution.

- **Implementation Techniques:**
  Step-by-step approaches to building and testing multi-robot systems.

- **Real-World Applications:**
  Case studies in industrial automation, search and rescue, and autonomous delivery.

- **Challenges and Future Directions:**
  Strategies to overcome common pitfalls and a look ahead at emerging trends.

Rhetorical Question:

Are you ready to harness the collective power of multi-robot systems and collaborative robotics to create solutions that not only enhance efficiency but also redefine the possibilities of automation? The future is collaborative, and it's waiting for innovative minds like yours.

Final Words of Encouragement

Every great technological breakthrough starts with a single idea and grows through collaboration. By leveraging multi-robot systems, you can multiply the capabilities of individual robots, creating a network of intelligent, responsive, and adaptive machines that work together seamlessly. Remember:

- **Innovation is a Team Effort:**
  Just as in any human endeavor, teamwork is key. Your ability to design systems where robots collaborate effectively will be a cornerstone of future breakthroughs.

- **Continuous Improvement is Vital:**
  Embrace iterative development, rigorous testing, and real-world feedback to refine your systems continually.

- **The Future is Now:**
  With the tools, strategies, and technologies at your

disposal, you're well-equipped to lead the charge into an era where collaborative robotics transforms industries and improves lives.

Rhetorical Question:

Imagine a world where every task—from manufacturing and logistics to healthcare and urban management—is executed by a harmonious network of robots, each contributing its unique strengths to a greater whole. Isn't that a future worth building?

---

10. Resources for Further Exploration

To continue your journey into multi-robot systems and collaborative robotics, here are some resources that can provide further insights and practical tools:

Books and Publications

- **"Distributed Autonomous Robotic Systems"** - Explore various architectures and case studies on multi-robot collaboration.

- **"Swarm Robotics: From Biology to Robotics"** - Delve into the principles of swarm intelligence and how they apply to robotics.

- **"Cooperative Control of Multi-Agent Systems"** - Learn about control algorithms and coordination strategies for groups of robots.

Online Courses and Tutorials

- **Coursera and edX:**
  Look for courses on robotics, multi-agent systems, and distributed control.

- **ROS2 Tutorials:**
  Engage with the extensive ROS2 community and learn practical implementations for multi-robot communication and coordination.

Tools and Software

- **ROS2:**
  An essential middleware for multi-robot systems that offers robust communication and coordination capabilities.

- **Gazebo:**
  A powerful simulation environment to test and validate multi-robot strategies.

- **MATLAB/Simulink:**
  Useful for designing and simulating control systems and collaborative algorithms.

- **GitHub:**
  Explore open-source projects related to swarm robotics and collaborative systems to see how others are tackling similar challenges.

Communities and Conferences

- **IEEE Robotics and Automation Society:**
  A great platform to connect with professionals and stay updated on the latest research.

- **Robotics Meetups and Hackathons:**
  Engage with local and online communities to collaborate on projects and exchange ideas.

Rhetorical Question:
Wouldn't it be inspiring to connect with a global community of roboticists who are pushing the boundaries of what robots can achieve together? The more you learn and collaborate, the more innovative your solutions will become.

---

11. Final Reflective Thought

Multi-robot systems and collaborative robotics represent the future of automation—a future where machines not only work independently but also communicate, cooperate, and create value as a cohesive team. As you continue your journey, remember that every challenge you overcome and every system you build is a step toward a more interconnected, efficient, and intelligent world.

Take a moment to envision:

- A fleet of autonomous drones coordinating to deliver critical supplies during emergencies.

- A group of warehouse robots working in harmony to streamline logistics.

- Collaborative robots in a manufacturing line, each perfectly synchronizing with its peers to produce high-quality products with unmatched precision.

These aren't just dreams—they're the reality of collaborative robotics. And you have the skills and knowledge to be at the forefront of this revolution.

12. Conclusion: The Journey Ahead

In this chapter, we've covered everything you need to know about multi-robot systems and collaborative robotics—from fundamental concepts and communication strategies to real-world applications and future trends. You've learned how to design systems where robots work together seamlessly, ensuring efficiency, resilience, and innovation.

As you move forward, remember:

- **Collaboration is Key:**
  Just as teams of people achieve great things by working together, robots too can unlock unprecedented potential when they collaborate.

- **Adaptability is Essential:**
  The field of robotics is ever-evolving, and the ability to adapt to new challenges and integrate emerging technologies will set your work apart.

- **Your Contribution Matters:**
  Whether you're developing a small fleet of service robots or a vast swarm for industrial applications, every project pushes the boundaries of what's possible.

Rhetorical Question:
Are you ready to build the future of robotics—one where collaboration isn't just a feature but the very foundation of intelligent systems? The road ahead is full of challenges, but it's also brimming with opportunities for those who dare to innovate.

Final Words

Multi-robot systems and collaborative robotics are not just technological advancements—they're a paradigm shift. They embody the idea that together, machines can achieve what no single unit ever could. As you embark on your projects, let the principles outlined in this chapter guide you. Build, test, refine, and iterate. Embrace the collaborative spirit, and let your systems be a testament to what can be achieved when intelligence meets teamwork.

Happy building, and here's to a future where every robot is a vital member of a greater, collaborative whole!

Chapter 9: Real-World Applications and Case Studies

Welcome to a deep dive into the realm where theory meets practice—where intelligent robotics transcends the laboratory and transforms industries, communities, and lives. In this chapter, we explore real-world applications and case studies that exemplify the immense potential of robotics. From manufacturing floors to disaster zones, and from healthcare innovations to space exploration, we'll break down how robotics systems are being deployed, the challenges they overcome, and the benefits they deliver. Whether you're a seasoned professional or an enthusiastic newcomer, this guide will provide clear, actionable insights into the transformative power of robotics in the real world.

Throughout this chapter, we maintain a focus on clarity—every technical term is explained in simple language, and each section is broken down into step-by-step approaches and bullet lists. We'll also include diagrams to visually represent workflows and concepts, ensuring you can follow along with ease.

Rhetorical Question:
Have you ever wondered how a fleet of autonomous robots can assemble a car with unparalleled precision or how a

rescue robot navigates through rubble to save lives? Let's find out!

---

1. Introduction: Bridging the Gap Between Concept and Reality

Before we explore specific case studies, it's essential to understand why real-world applications matter. While theoretical models and simulations provide a strong foundation, they're only the starting point. Real-world deployments validate those models under unpredictable conditions, uncover new challenges, and drive continuous innovation.

1.1 The Significance of Real-World Deployments

Real-world applications push the limits of robotics technology:

- **Validation of Technology:**
  Field tests reveal how systems perform under stress, unexpected conditions, and dynamic environments.

- **Driving Innovation:**
  Challenges encountered in real-world scenarios spark new ideas and technological breakthroughs.

- **Economic Impact:**
  Successful robotics deployments can reduce costs, increase productivity, and create new markets.

- **Improving Quality of Life:**
  From medical robots that assist in surgeries to delivery drones that bring essentials to remote areas, robotics is making a tangible difference.

1.2 A Roadmap to Our Case Studies

In this chapter, we'll cover:

- Industrial Automation in Manufacturing

- Autonomous Delivery Systems in Urban Settings

- Healthcare Robotics Transforming Patient Care

- Disaster Response and Search & Rescue Operations

- Agriculture Robotics for Sustainable Farming

- Space Exploration: Robotics Beyond Earth

- Collaborative Systems in Smart Cities

Each section will provide:

- A detailed explanation of the application.

- A step-by-step guide outlining how the technology is implemented.

- A diagram to visually represent the workflow or architecture.

- Real-world examples and outcomes.

---

2. Industrial Automation in Manufacturing

Industrial automation has long been a cornerstone of modern manufacturing. Today, robotics takes automation to new heights by integrating intelligent decision-making, collaborative operation, and precision control.

2.1 Overview of Industrial Automation

In a modern factory, robots work side by side with humans and other machines to assemble products, manage inventory, and optimize production lines. These systems enhance efficiency, reduce errors, and ensure consistency.

Real-World Example:
Consider a smart factory where robotic arms assemble automotive components with extreme precision while mobile robots transport parts between stations.

2.2 Step-by-Step Implementation in Manufacturing

Step 1: Define the Production Process

- **Action:**
  Map out the entire manufacturing process from raw material intake to finished product.

- **Tip:**
  Identify repetitive tasks that could be automated.

Step 2: Identify Key Tasks for Automation

- **Tasks:**

  - Welding and assembly

  - Painting and coating

  - Material transport and logistics

  - Quality inspection

Step 3: Deploy Specialized Robots

- **Action:**
  Assign different robots to different tasks. For example:

  - **Robotic Arms:** Handle welding, painting, and assembly.

  - **Mobile Robots:** Transport parts between workstations.

  - **Inspection Robots:** Use cameras and sensors for quality control.

Step 4: Integrate Control Systems

- **Action:**
  Use centralized or decentralized control systems (often using ROS2) to coordinate tasks.

- **Tip:**
  Ensure that each robot communicates its status and receives commands in real time.

Step 5: Implement Safety and Redundancy Measures

- **Action:**
  Integrate safety protocols, emergency stops, and redundancy strategies.

- **Tip:**
  Test the system rigorously under simulated failure conditions.

Rhetorical Question:
Can you envision a factory where robots seamlessly pass parts between one another, each performing its specialized task with unmatched precision and speed? That's the future of industrial automation.

2.3 Case Study: The Smart Automotive Factory

Scenario:
A leading automotive manufacturer integrates a fleet of robotic arms, mobile transport robots, and inspection systems to automate its assembly line.

Implementation Details:

1. **Task Identification:**

- o Robotic arms are programmed for welding and assembly.

- o Mobile robots manage the logistics of transporting heavy components.

- o Inspection systems with high-resolution cameras verify the quality of welds and assemblies.

2. **Control and Coordination:**

   - o A centralized control system coordinates the timing and flow of parts.

   - o Safety protocols ensure that any malfunction triggers an immediate halt to prevent accidents.

3. **Results:**

   - o Production efficiency increased by 30%.

   - o Error rates reduced by 25%.

   - o The system's adaptability allowed for rapid reconfiguration for different car models.

Rhetorical Question:
Imagine a production line that adapts in real time to changing demands, significantly cutting down waste and errors—this is not a distant dream but an achievable reality in modern manufacturing.

3. Autonomous Delivery Systems in Urban Environments

Urban logistics have been transformed by autonomous delivery systems. These systems use a combination of ground robots and aerial drones to deliver packages, food, and essential supplies quickly and efficiently.

3.1 Overview of Autonomous Delivery

Autonomous delivery systems are designed to navigate complex urban landscapes, avoiding obstacles, adapting to traffic patterns, and ensuring timely delivery. They harness advanced navigation, sensor fusion, and real-time decision-making.

Real-World Example:
A fleet of delivery robots in a bustling city can autonomously navigate sidewalks, cross streets safely, and deliver packages directly to customers' doorsteps.

3.2 Step-by-Step Implementation for Urban Delivery

Step 1: Define the Delivery Route

- **Action:**
  Map out typical urban routes including pedestrian areas, intersections, and delivery points.

- **Tip:**
  Use historical data and real-time traffic updates to plan optimal routes.

Step 2: Equip Robots with Essential Sensors

- **Sensors:**

    o LIDAR for obstacle detection

    o Cameras for navigation

    o GPS for global positioning (supplemented by local beacons in dense areas)

- **Action:**
  Install and calibrate sensors to ensure accurate perception.

Step 3: Develop a Robust Navigation Algorithm

- **Algorithm:**
  Implement SLAM for mapping and localization.

- **Action:**
  Continuously update the map as the robot moves through dynamic environments.

Step 4: Integrate Communication Systems

- **Action:**
  Enable robots to share traffic data, obstacle information, and delivery statuses using ROS2 topics.

- **Tip:**
  Consider both centralized coordination (a control hub) and decentralized communication for scalability.

Step 5: Implement Safety and Redundancy Protocols

- **Action:**
  Use real-time monitoring to detect potential hazards and trigger evasive maneuvers.

- **Tip:**
  Incorporate fallback strategies such as returning to a safe zone if communication is lost.

3.3 Case Study: Urban Delivery Fleet

Scenario:
A major logistics company deploys a fleet of autonomous delivery robots across a metropolitan area.

Implementation Details:

1. **Route Optimization:**
   - Robots use real-time traffic data and predictive algorithms to avoid congested areas.

2. **Sensor Integration:**
   - LIDAR and cameras work in tandem to navigate crowded sidewalks and dynamic urban obstacles.

3. **Inter-Robot Communication:**

- ○ Robots share data to avoid collisions and reassign deliveries if one encounters a delay.

4. **Results:**

- ○ Delivery times reduced by 40%.

- ○ Operational costs dropped by 35%.

- ○ Customer satisfaction ratings improved significantly due to timely deliveries.

Rhetorical Question:
Imagine receiving your package not hours later, but within minutes of placing your order—autonomous delivery systems are turning this vision into reality, revolutionizing urban logistics one street at a time.

4. Healthcare Robotics: Transforming Patient Care

Healthcare is one of the most impactful fields for robotics, where precision, reliability, and compassion are paramount. Robots in healthcare assist in surgeries, manage patient care, and provide support in rehabilitation.

4.1 Overview of Healthcare Robotics

Healthcare robotics spans a wide range of applications:

- **Surgical Robots:**
  Enhance precision in delicate procedures.

- **Rehabilitation Robots:**
  Assist patients in regaining mobility and strength.

- **Telepresence Robots:**
  Enable remote consultations and monitoring.

- **Service Robots:**
  Manage logistics in hospitals, such as delivering medications and supplies.

Real-World Example:
A surgical robot performs minimally invasive procedures with unmatched precision, reducing recovery times and improving patient outcomes.

4.2 Step-by-Step Implementation in Healthcare

Step 1: Define the Medical Application

- **Action:**
  Identify the specific healthcare need—whether it's surgery, rehabilitation, or patient monitoring.

- **Tip:**
  Collaborate with medical professionals to understand the requirements and constraints.

Step 2: Design the Robotic System

- **Components:**
  - Precision instruments (for surgical robots)
  - Exoskeletons (for rehabilitation robots)

- o Telepresence interfaces (for remote consultations)

- **Action:**
Develop prototypes that meet the clinical requirements.

Step 3: Integrate Sensor and Control Systems

- **Action:**
Equip the robot with sensors (e.g., force sensors, cameras) and advanced control algorithms to ensure safe and precise operations.

- **Tip:**
Prioritize safety and reliability in every design phase.

Step 4: Validate Through Simulations and Trials

- **Action:**
Run extensive simulations, followed by clinical trials, to ensure the system performs as intended.

- **Tip:**
Gather feedback from medical professionals and iterate on the design.

4.4 Case Study: Robotic Surgical Assistant

Scenario:
A renowned hospital deploys a robotic surgical assistant to enhance minimally invasive procedures.

Implementation Details:

1. **Collaboration with Surgeons:**

   o Gather requirements and design specifications directly from medical experts.

2. **Precision Instrumentation:**

   o The robot is equipped with high-resolution cameras and force feedback sensors.

3. **Control Algorithms:**

   o Advanced control systems enable fine movements and real-time adjustments during surgery.

4. **Clinical Trials:**

   o Extensive testing shows reduced surgery times and improved patient outcomes.

5. **Results:**

   o Enhanced surgical precision, lower complication rates, and faster patient recovery.

Rhetorical Question:

Can you imagine the profound impact on patient care when a robot can assist surgeons with pinpoint accuracy, reducing risks and speeding up recovery? Healthcare robotics is not just about technology—it's about saving lives.

5. Disaster Response and Search & Rescue

In times of crisis, robots can make the difference between life and death. Disaster response and search & rescue (SAR) operations are some of the most challenging yet rewarding applications of robotics.

5.1 Overview of Robotics in Disaster Response

Robots deployed in disaster scenarios are designed to:

- **Navigate Hazardous Environments:**
  Traverse debris, unstable structures, and dangerous terrain.

- **Locate Survivors:**
  Use sensors and cameras to identify human presence.

- **Deliver Aid:**
  Transport essential supplies to areas that are otherwise inaccessible.

- **Gather Critical Data:**
  Map affected areas to guide rescue operations.

Real-World Example:
After a natural disaster, a fleet of drones and ground robots can work together to locate survivors, provide real-time mapping, and even deliver first aid supplies.

5.2 Step-by-Step Implementation for SAR

Step 1: Define the Mission Scope

- **Action:**
  Identify the disaster scenario and the specific tasks the robots must perform.

- **Tip:**
  Focus on critical tasks such as search, mapping, and supply delivery.

Step 2: Equip Robots with Specialized Sensors

- **Sensors:**

  - Thermal cameras for detecting human heat signatures

  - LIDAR for mapping and obstacle avoidance

  - GPS and inertial sensors for accurate positioning

- **Action:**
  Ensure robust sensor integration for reliable performance in chaotic environments.

Step 3: Develop Robust Navigation and Mapping Algorithms

- **Action:**
  Implement SLAM algorithms adapted to dynamic, cluttered environments.

- **Tip:**
  Use real-time data processing to update maps continuously.

Step 4: Coordinate Multi-Robot Operations

- **Action:**
  Use decentralized coordination to allow robots to cover different areas without overlap.

- **Tip:**
  Implement fallback protocols to reassign tasks if a robot fails or becomes obstructed.

Step 5: Test in Simulated Disaster Scenarios

- **Action:**
  Use simulation tools to recreate disaster environments and validate robot performance.

- **Tip:**
  Conduct field tests when possible to simulate real-world challenges.

5.3 Case Study: Swarm Robotics in Disaster Relief

Scenario:
In the aftermath of an earthquake, a swarm of aerial drones and ground robots is deployed to search for survivors and assess structural damage.

Implementation Details:

1. **Mission Definition:**

   o Focus on search operations and real-time mapping.

2. **Sensor Deployment:**

   o Drones are equipped with thermal imaging, while ground robots use LIDAR and cameras.

3. **Coordination Protocols:**

   o Robots communicate over a robust, decentralized network to avoid interference.

4. **Outcomes:**

   o The system locates survivors faster than traditional methods.

   o Rescue teams receive accurate maps of the affected area, enabling more efficient rescue operations.

Rhetorical Question:

Imagine the difference in rescue operations when robots can navigate dangerous terrain and locate survivors quickly—this is the transformative potential of robotics in disaster response.

6. Agriculture Robotics for Sustainable Farming

Agriculture is undergoing a revolution as robotics takes center stage in achieving sustainable, efficient, and productive farming practices. From planting to harvesting, robots are enhancing every stage of the agricultural process.

6.1 Overview of Robotics in Agriculture

Modern farming faces challenges such as labor shortages, climate change, and the need for increased efficiency. Robotics addresses these issues by:

- **Automating Repetitive Tasks:**
  Robots can plant seeds, water crops, and harvest produce.

- **Precision Farming:**
  Using sensors and data analytics to optimize resource usage.

- **Monitoring Crop Health:**
  Drones and ground robots can detect pest infestations and nutrient deficiencies in real time.

Real-World Example:
An agricultural robot equipped with multispectral cameras surveys fields to identify areas of stress in crops, allowing farmers to target interventions precisely where needed.

6.2 Step-by-Step Implementation in Agriculture

Step 1: Define the Agricultural Task

- **Action:**
  Determine which farming tasks will benefit most from automation (e.g., harvesting, weeding).

- **Tip:**
  Prioritize tasks that are labor-intensive or require high precision.

Step 2: Equip Robots with Necessary Tools and Sensors

- **Sensors:**

  - Multispectral cameras for crop health analysis

  - Soil moisture sensors

  - GPS for precise field navigation

- **Action:**
  Ensure that robots are rugged and capable of operating in outdoor environments.

Step 3: Develop Precision Control Algorithms

- **Action:**
  Implement control systems that allow robots to navigate irregular terrain and adjust to varying crop conditions.

- **Tip:**
  Use feedback from sensors to dynamically adjust operations.

Step 4: Integrate Data Analytics for Decision-Making

- **Action:**
  Collect data over time to predict crop yields and optimize planting strategies.

- **Tip:**
  Use cloud-based analytics for real-time insights.

6.3 Case Study: Autonomous Harvesting Robot

Scenario:
A large-scale farm deploys autonomous harvesting robots that can selectively pick ripe produce, reducing waste and increasing efficiency.

Implementation Details:

1. **Task Definition:**
   - Focus on fruit picking in orchards.

2. **Sensor Integration:**
   - Robots use cameras and spectral sensors to assess fruit ripeness.

3. **Precision Control:**

- o Advanced algorithms guide the robot's arm for gentle but effective harvesting.

4. **Results:**

- o Harvest times reduced by 50%.

- o Labor costs decreased significantly.

- o Consistent quality of produce improved overall market value.

Rhetorical Question:
Wouldn't it be revolutionary to see robots that not only increase yield but also ensure that every piece of fruit is picked at the perfect moment? Agriculture robotics is paving the way for a sustainable future in farming.

---

7. Space Exploration Robotics: Reaching Beyond Earth

Space exploration has always pushed the limits of technology, and robotics is at the forefront of these endeavors. Robots in space are designed to operate in extreme conditions, explore distant planets, and perform tasks that are too risky for humans.

7.1 Overview of Space Robotics

Space robotics involves the development of machines that can:

- **Explore Uncharted Territories:**
  Traverse the rugged landscapes of Mars, the Moon, and beyond.

- **Conduct Scientific Experiments:**
  Collect samples, analyze geological data, and perform in-situ experiments.

- **Maintain and Repair Spacecraft:**
  Assist with satellite repairs and even construction in orbit.

Real-World Example:
The Mars rovers, such as Curiosity and Perseverance, are prime examples of advanced space robotics. They navigate the Martian surface, collect valuable data, and even prepare for future human exploration.

7.2 Step-by-Step Implementation for Space Exploration

Step 1: Define Mission Objectives

- **Action:**
  Determine the scientific and operational goals (e.g., sample collection, terrain mapping).

- **Tip:**
  Collaborate with scientists to understand the mission requirements.

Step 2: Design a Robust Robotic Platform

- **Components:**

    - ○ Durable chassis and wheels/tracks for rugged terrain

    - ○ Advanced sensor suite (cameras, spectrometers, environmental sensors)

- **Action:**
  Develop a model that can withstand extreme temperatures, dust, and radiation.

Step 3: Implement Autonomous Navigation

- **Action:**
  Use SLAM and machine learning techniques to enable the rover to navigate unknown terrain.

- **Tip:**
  Simulate the environment extensively on Earth before deployment.

Step 4: Integrate Communication Systems

- **Action:**
  Ensure reliable communication with Earth, accounting for signal delays.

- **Tip:**
  Use relay satellites or high-gain antennas for robust data transmission.

7.3 Case Study: Mars Rover Missions

Scenario:

NASA's Mars rovers have revolutionized our understanding of the Red Planet by collecting geological data, capturing high-resolution images, and even preparing for human missions.

Implementation Details:

1. **Mission Objectives:**

   o Explore the Martian surface for signs of water and past life.

2. **Platform Design:**

   o Rovers are built to endure harsh Martian conditions.

3. **Autonomous Navigation:**

   o Advanced algorithms enable the rover to navigate rocky, unpredictable terrain.

4. **Communication:**

   o Data is relayed back to Earth through a network of orbiters.

5. **Results:**

   o Groundbreaking discoveries about Mars' geology and climate.

   o Valuable insights for future manned missions.

Rhetorical Question:
Imagine a machine that can traverse alien landscapes, uncovering the secrets of another planet—this is the awe-inspiring reality of space exploration robotics.

---

8. Collaborative Systems in Smart Cities

Smart cities represent the convergence of technology and urban planning, where interconnected systems improve efficiency, safety, and quality of life. In this section, we explore how collaborative robotics plays a pivotal role in creating the cities of the future.

8.1 Overview of Smart City Applications

In smart cities, robotics is used to:

- **Optimize Traffic Management:**
  Autonomous vehicles and drones coordinate to manage traffic flow.

- **Enhance Public Safety:**
  Surveillance and emergency response robots assist law enforcement.

- **Improve Urban Infrastructure:**
  Robots maintain public spaces, monitor environmental conditions, and manage waste.

- **Facilitate Last-Mile Delivery:**
  Delivery robots ensure efficient logistics in dense urban areas.

Real-World Example:
A city deploys a fleet of autonomous maintenance robots that monitor infrastructure, perform repairs, and coordinate with municipal services in real time.

8.2 Step-by-Step Implementation for Collaborative Smart City Systems

Step 1: Define Urban Challenges

- **Action:**
  Identify key areas where robotics can improve urban living (e.g., traffic, waste management, public safety).

- **Tip:**
  Use data analytics to pinpoint the most critical issues.

Step 2: Deploy a Network of Robots

- **Action:**
  Equip the city with various types of robots (e.g., surveillance drones, maintenance bots, delivery robots).

- **Tip:**
  Ensure interoperability through standardized communication protocols.

Step 3: Integrate Centralized and Decentralized Systems

- **Action:**
  Use a hybrid approach where a central control system coordinates city-wide operations, while individual robots handle local tasks autonomously.

- **Tip:**
  Implement robust cybersecurity measures to protect data and operations.

Step 4: Monitor and Optimize

- **Action:**
  Continuously collect data on system performance and adjust operations as needed.

- **Tip:**
  Use digital twins to simulate and optimize urban processes.

8.3 Case Study: Smart City Logistics and Maintenance

Scenario:
A major metropolitan area implements a smart city initiative that integrates autonomous delivery robots, maintenance drones, and surveillance systems to streamline urban operations.

Implementation Details:

1. **Challenge Identification:**

- o Traffic congestion, delayed maintenance, and inefficient logistics.

2. **Deployment:**

   - o Autonomous delivery robots handle last-mile logistics.

   - o Maintenance drones inspect infrastructure and perform minor repairs.

   - o Surveillance systems ensure public safety.

3. **Coordination:**

   - o A central control hub integrates data from all systems, enabling real-time adjustments.

4. **Results:**

   - o Traffic flow improved by 20%, maintenance response times decreased significantly, and overall urban efficiency increased.

5. **Lessons Learned:**

   - o Effective integration and real-time data analytics are critical for success.

Rhetorical Question:
Can you imagine living in a city where every aspect of urban life—from traffic to public safety—is optimized by a network of intelligent, collaborative robots? That's the promise of smart city robotics.

9. Conclusion: Lessons Learned from Real-World Applications

Real-world applications and case studies illustrate the transformative power of robotics across various industries. The projects and systems we've explored in this chapter demonstrate that when intelligent design meets practical implementation, the results are nothing short of revolutionary.

9.1 Recap of Key Insights

- **Industrial Automation:**
  Collaborative robots have revolutionized manufacturing by increasing efficiency and reducing errors.

- **Autonomous Delivery:**
  Urban delivery systems leverage advanced navigation and communication to ensure timely and efficient logistics.

- **Healthcare Robotics:**
  Precision and reliability in robotics are reshaping patient care and surgical procedures.

- **Disaster Response:**
  Multi-robot systems are saving lives by swiftly navigating hazardous environments and assisting in rescue operations.

- **Agriculture Robotics:**
  Automation in farming enhances productivity and
  sustainability through precision and real-time data
  analysis.

- **Space Exploration:**
  Robotic explorers are unlocking the secrets of distant
  planets, paving the way for human exploration.

- **Smart City Collaboration:**
  Integrated robotics systems are transforming urban
  life, making cities more efficient, safe, and responsive.

9.2 Your Path Forward

As you reflect on these case studies, consider how the
principles and techniques discussed can be applied to your
projects. Here are some next steps:

1. **Experiment with Real-World Deployments:**

   o Start with pilot projects in controlled
      environments.

2. **Leverage Simulation and Digital Twins:**

   o Validate your designs using simulations before
      real-world implementation.

3. **Engage with Industry Experts:**

   o Collaborate with professionals and researchers
      to refine your systems.

4. **Focus on Continuous Improvement:**

- o Use feedback from real-world deployments to iterate and enhance system performance.

5. **Document and Share Your Findings:**

- o Contribute to the robotics community by publishing case studies and sharing insights.

Rhetorical Question:

Are you ready to take the leap from theory to practice and harness the full potential of robotics to solve real-world challenges? The case studies in this chapter prove that the future is already here—now it's up to you to shape it.

10. Final Words: Shaping a Better Future Through Robotics

Real-world applications and case studies are more than just success stories—they're blueprints for the future. They show us that robotics is not confined to the pages of textbooks or the controlled environment of labs; it's a dynamic force that can transform industries, improve lives, and drive economic growth.

Key Takeaways:

- **Innovation Through Collaboration:**
  Multi-robot systems and collaborative robotics multiply individual strengths, leading to systems that are greater than the sum of their parts.

- **Practical Impact:**
  Whether it's enhancing production lines, saving lives
  in disaster scenarios, or making cities smarter, robotics
  is making a measurable difference.

- **Continuous Evolution:**
  The field of robotics is in constant flux, with new
  technologies and methodologies emerging every day.
  Staying informed and adaptable is key to success.

Looking Ahead

As you continue your journey in robotics, remember that the
case studies presented here are just the beginning. The
challenges and opportunities are vast, and with every project,
you have the chance to contribute to a more efficient,
sustainable, and innovative world. Whether you're building
systems for industrial automation, urban logistics, healthcare,
or any other field, your work will help shape the future of
technology.

Final Reflective Thought:
Picture a world where every challenge is met with a robotic
solution—a world where technology and human ingenuity
work in harmony to overcome obstacles and create a better,
more connected society. This is not a distant dream but a
reality that you can help build, one project at a time.

Rhetorical Question:
Will you be the innovator who transforms challenges into

opportunities, harnessing the power of robotics to create a future that is not only smarter but also more humane?

---

11. Conclusion: The Journey Continues

Real-world applications and case studies are the lifeblood of robotics innovation. They bridge the gap between theory and practice, turning ideas into tangible, impactful solutions. In this chapter, we've journeyed through the transformative potential of robotics across industries—from manufacturing and urban delivery to healthcare, disaster response, agriculture, space exploration, and smart cities.

You've seen how advanced systems are designed, implemented, and optimized to meet real-world challenges. More importantly, you've learned that every case study is not just a story of success—it's a lesson, a blueprint, and an inspiration for your next breakthrough.

As you move forward:

- **Embrace Collaboration:**
  Whether you're working with a team of robots or a team of innovators, collaboration is the key to unlocking new possibilities.

- **Pursue Continuous Improvement:**
  Each project, each challenge, and each success is a stepping stone to greater innovation.

- **Stay Curious and Resilient:**
  The world of robotics is constantly evolving. Keep learning, keep experimenting, and never stop pushing the boundaries of what's possible.

Final Reflective Thought:
In a world where technology is rapidly reshaping our lives, robotics stands as a testament to human ingenuity—a field where every challenge inspires a solution, and every system built today lays the foundation for the breakthroughs of tomorrow.

Rhetorical Question:
Are you ready to be a part of that future, to design systems that not only meet the demands of today but also pave the way for a smarter, more connected tomorrow?

Happy innovating, and here's to a future where real-world robotics applications continue to transform our world in ways we can only begin to imagine!

Chapter 10: Debugging, Testing, and Troubleshooting

Welcome to one of the most critical aspects of robotics and software development—debugging, testing, and troubleshooting. In this chapter, we'll guide you through the processes of identifying, diagnosing, and fixing issues in your systems. Whether you're a seasoned developer or just starting out, effective debugging and testing can mean the difference between a project that performs flawlessly and one that falls short under pressure. We'll break down each step in clear, jargon-free language, use relatable analogies to make complex concepts approachable, and provide actionable steps, complete with diagrams, to ensure that you can master these skills.

Imagine you're a detective in a high-stakes mystery where every clue counts. Your code is your case file, and debugging is the process of piecing together evidence to solve the mystery of what went wrong. Testing and troubleshooting are your tools for ensuring that every line of code works as intended, just as a detective double-checks every lead to make sure nothing is overlooked.

Let's dive in and explore how to debug, test, and troubleshoot like a tech pro!

1. Introduction: The Importance of Debugging, Testing, and Troubleshooting

Before any code runs flawlessly in a production environment, it must be rigorously tested and debugged. Debugging, testing, and troubleshooting are the unsung heroes of development—they ensure that your systems are robust, reliable, and ready for real-world deployment.

1.1 Why These Processes Matter

- **Reliability:**
  Systems that have been thoroughly debugged and tested are more dependable, reducing downtime and costly errors.

- **User Experience:**
  A smooth, bug-free application leads to happier users and better adoption.

- **Efficiency:**
  Early detection and resolution of issues save time and resources in the long run.

- **Continuous Improvement:**
  Debugging and testing are part of an iterative process, constantly refining your system and paving the way for future enhancements.

Rhetorical Question:

Have you ever encountered a system that crashes unexpectedly or behaves erratically, leaving you frustrated and uncertain? Effective debugging and testing transform that chaos into a smooth, predictable performance.

1.2 What This Chapter Covers

In this chapter, you will learn:

- **Debugging Techniques:**
  Step-by-step methods to identify and fix errors in your code.

- **Testing Methodologies:**
  A systematic approach to validating the performance and reliability of your system.

- **Troubleshooting Strategies:**
  How to approach complex problems methodically to find root causes and resolve issues.

- **Best Practices and Tools:**
  Recommended tools and practices that streamline the debugging and testing process.

- **Real-World Case Studies:**
  Examples that illustrate these concepts in action, giving you practical insights into solving real challenges.

2. Debugging Techniques and Strategies

Debugging is the process of finding and fixing errors or "bugs" in your code. Think of it as the meticulous work of a detective, where every clue—every log, every output—leads you closer to the solution. Debugging techniques can vary from simple print statements to sophisticated debugging tools that allow you to inspect variables, trace function calls, and monitor the state of your system in real time.

2.1 Step-by-Step Debugging Approach

Step 1: Reproduce the Problem

- **Action:**
  Ensure that you can reliably reproduce the error. This might involve running the program with specific inputs or under certain conditions.

- **Why It Matters:**
  If you can't consistently recreate the problem, diagnosing it becomes much harder.

Step 2: Isolate the Error

- **Action:**
  Narrow down the part of your code where the error occurs. This can be achieved by:

  - Adding print/log statements at critical points.

- Using breakpoints to pause execution and inspect the state.

- **Tip:**
  Simplify your code if possible, and comment out sections until the error disappears. This "divide and conquer" method helps pinpoint the source.

Step 3: Analyze the Error

- **Action:**
  Read error messages carefully—they often contain valuable clues about what went wrong. Look for:

  - The type of error (e.g., syntax error, runtime error, logic error).

  - The specific location in your code where the error occurred.

- **Tip:**
  Use online resources and forums like Stack Overflow to research error messages you don't understand.

Step 4: Develop a Hypothesis

- **Action:**
  Based on the information gathered, form a theory about what might be causing the error.

- **Example:**
  If a variable is not updating as expected, hypothesize that there may be a scope issue or an unintended mutation.

Step 5: Test Your Hypothesis

- **Action:**
  Modify your code in a small, controlled way to test whether your hypothesis is correct.

- **Tip:**
  Use unit tests or temporary print statements to verify your assumptions.

Step 6: Implement the Fix and Verify

- **Action:**
  Once the cause is identified, implement a solution and run your tests again to confirm that the error is resolved.

- **Tip:**
  Ensure that the fix does not introduce new issues; consider writing regression tests.

2.2 Debugging Tools and Techniques

While manual debugging with print statements is sometimes effective, modern development environments offer powerful tools to streamline the process.

Integrated Development Environment (IDE) Debuggers

- **Features:**
  - Set breakpoints
  - Step through code line by line
  - Inspect variables and call stacks in real time

- **Examples:**

  - Visual Studio Code, PyCharm, Eclipse

Logging

- **Purpose:**
  Logging allows you to record events and errors during execution, providing a history of what happened leading up to an error.

- **Best Practices:**

  - Use different logging levels (DEBUG, INFO, WARNING, ERROR)

  - Log messages should be clear and concise

- **Tip:**
  Configure your logging system to write to a file for later analysis.

Profiling Tools

- **Purpose:**
  Profilers help you understand performance bottlenecks in your code.

- **Examples:**

  - cProfile for Python, VisualVM for Java

- **Tip:**
  Use profilers in conjunction with debugging to optimize both correctness and performance.

Rhetorical Question:
Have you ever felt like you were chasing a ghost in your code? A systematic debugging approach is your flashlight in the dark, illuminating the path to a solution.

---

3. Testing Methodologies: Ensuring Code Quality

Testing is the practice of executing your code with the intent of finding errors and verifying that it behaves as expected. A robust testing strategy is essential to catch issues early, ensure reliability, and build confidence in your system.

3.1 Types of Testing

1. Unit Testing:

- **Definition:**
  Testing individual components or functions in isolation.

- **Example:**
  Testing a function that calculates the area of a circle to ensure it returns the correct value for various inputs.

- **Actionable Steps:**

  1. Identify functions or modules to test.

  2. Write test cases for each function.

  3. Use testing frameworks like PyTest or unittest.

2. Integration Testing:

- **Definition:**
  Testing the interactions between different components or modules.

- **Example:**
  Verifying that a data processing module correctly passes data to a visualization module.

- **Actionable Steps:**

  1. Identify module interfaces.

  2. Write test cases that simulate interactions.

  3. Ensure that data flows correctly between components.

3. System Testing:

- **Definition:**
  Testing the entire system as a whole to ensure that it meets the specified requirements.

- **Example:**
  Running a full simulation of a robot performing a task to check overall performance.

- **Actionable Steps:**

  1. Define end-to-end test scenarios.

  2. Execute tests in an environment that mimics real-world conditions.

3. Validate that the system performs as expected.

4. Acceptance Testing:

- **Definition:**
  Testing the system with real users to ensure it meets their needs and expectations.

- **Example:**
  Conducting user trials for a customer service chatbot.

- **Actionable Steps:**

  1. Define acceptance criteria.

  2. Gather user feedback during testing.

  3. Iterate based on user input.

3.2 Step-by-Step Testing Approach

Step 1: Write Clear Test Cases

- **Action:**
  Document what each test case should accomplish, including input, expected output, and steps to execute.

- **Tip:**
  Use a standard format to maintain consistency.

Step 2: Automate Your Tests

- **Action:**
  Use testing frameworks to automate repetitive tests.

- **Examples:**

- o   PyTest for Python, JUnit for Java.

- **Tip:**
  Integrate tests into your CI/CD pipeline to run them automatically with every code change.

Step 3: Run Tests Frequently

- **Action:**
  Test your code regularly during development to catch issues early.

- **Tip:**
  Adopt a test-driven development (TDD) approach where tests are written before code implementation.

Step 4: Analyze Test Results

- **Action:**
  Review failed tests to understand why they failed.

- **Tip:**
  Use debugging tools to step through the test execution if necessary.

Step 5: Refactor and Retest

- **Action:**
  Make necessary changes to your code and run tests again until they pass.

- **Tip:**
  Keep tests small and focused for easier troubleshooting.

Rhetorical Question:
Wouldn't it be fantastic to catch errors before they reach production, ensuring a smooth and reliable user experience every time? Systematic testing is the secret to achieving that goal.

---

4. Troubleshooting: A Systematic Approach to Problem-Solving

Troubleshooting is the art of diagnosing and resolving issues that arise during development or deployment. It's like being a doctor for your code—identifying symptoms, determining the root cause, and administering the right treatment.

4.1 Step-by-Step Troubleshooting Process

Step 1: Gather Information

- **Action:**
  Collect all relevant data about the problem, including error messages, logs, and the context in which the error occurs.

- **Tip:**
  Ask questions: When does the error occur? What inputs trigger it? Is it reproducible?

Step 2: Isolate the Problem

- **Action:**
  Narrow down the scope to the specific module or function causing the issue.

- **Tip:**
  Disable or bypass parts of the system to see if the error persists.

Step 3: Formulate Hypotheses

- **Action:**
  Based on the collected data, propose possible causes of the issue.

- **Tip:**
  Consider both obvious and obscure possibilities, such as configuration errors or hardware malfunctions.

Step 4: Test Hypotheses

- **Action:**
  Implement small changes or run controlled tests to confirm or refute your theories.

- **Tip:**
  Keep detailed notes on what you tested and the outcomes.

Step 5: Apply the Fix and Monitor

- **Action:**
  Once you've identified the root cause, implement a solution.

- **Tip:**
  After applying the fix, monitor the system closely to ensure that the problem is truly resolved and that no new issues have emerged.

4.2 Tools for Troubleshooting

1. Log Analyzers:

- **Purpose:**
  Tools that parse and analyze log files to identify patterns and anomalies.

- **Examples:**
  - ELK Stack (Elasticsearch, Logstash, Kibana)
  - Splunk

2. Interactive Debuggers:

- **Purpose:**
  Step through code, inspect variables, and monitor the flow of execution in real time.

- **Examples:**
  - Python's pdb, Visual Studio Code Debugger

3. Profilers:

- **Purpose:**
  Analyze the performance of your code to detect bottlenecks and inefficient sections.

- **Examples:**

    ○ cProfile for Python, Perf for Linux

4. Monitoring Dashboards:

- **Purpose:**
  Visual tools that display real-time data about system performance, error rates, and resource usage.

- **Examples:**

      ○ Grafana, Prometheus

Rhetorical Question:
Have you ever felt overwhelmed by a persistent bug that just wouldn't go away? A structured troubleshooting process can turn that frustration into a clear path forward.

---

5. Best Practices for Debugging, Testing, and Troubleshooting

While having a systematic approach is crucial, following best practices can further enhance the effectiveness of your efforts. Here are some key guidelines:

5.1 Write Clean, Modular Code

- **Action:**
  Break your code into small, testable units.

- **Tip:**
  Use functions and modules to isolate functionality, making it easier to pinpoint errors.

5.2 Maintain Comprehensive Documentation

- **Action:**
  Document your code, test cases, and known issues.

- **Tip:**
  Keep a changelog and a troubleshooting guide that details past problems and solutions.

5.3 Use Version Control Effectively

- **Action:**
  Regularly commit your code and use branching to isolate experimental changes.

- **Tip:**
  Tools like Git allow you to revert to known good states, which is invaluable when debugging.

5.4 Automate Testing

- **Action:**
  Integrate unit, integration, and system tests into your development workflow.

- **Tip:**
  Continuous Integration (CI) tools like Jenkins or GitHub Actions can automatically run tests on every code commit.

5.5 Monitor System Performance

- **Action:**
  Set up dashboards and alerts to catch issues as soon as they occur.

- **Tip:**
  Use tools like Grafana and Prometheus to monitor performance metrics in real time.

Rhetorical Question:
Wouldn't it be empowering to know that your code is not only functional but also resilient, thanks to a disciplined approach to debugging and testing?

---

6. Real-World Case Studies in Debugging and Testing

To illustrate the impact of effective debugging, testing, and troubleshooting, let's explore a few real-world case studies where these practices made a significant difference.

6.1 Case Study: Autonomous Vehicle Software

Scenario:
An autonomous vehicle project encountered intermittent failures in obstacle detection, leading to unpredictable behavior in certain conditions.

Approach:

1. Problem Reproduction:

- Engineers simulated various driving scenarios in a virtual environment to reproduce the error.

2. Isolation:

- Using a combination of logging and breakpoints, they isolated the problem to a sensor fusion module.

3. Hypothesis Testing:

- Adjustments were made to the data weighting in the Kalman Filter algorithm.

4. Verification:

- Extensive field tests confirmed that the modifications led to more reliable obstacle detection.

5. Outcome:

- The fix improved detection accuracy by 20%, and the system's overall reliability increased significantly.

Rhetorical Question:
Imagine the confidence of knowing that even the most challenging issues in your autonomous vehicle software can be identified and resolved through systematic debugging. That's the power of a robust troubleshooting process.

6.2 Case Study: Industrial Robotics Quality Control

Scenario:
A manufacturing plant implemented robotics for quality control, but occasional discrepancies in sensor data led to faulty product inspections.

Approach:

1. **Data Collection:**
   - Detailed logs revealed that the sensor readings were inconsistent during high-speed operations.

2. **Isolation:**
   - Profiling tools pinpointed performance bottlenecks in the data processing pipeline.

3. **Hypothesis and Testing:**
   - Engineers optimized the data handling algorithm and introduced additional error-checking routines.

4. **Outcome:**
   - Quality control accuracy improved by 15%, reducing production errors and increasing throughput.

Rhetorical Question:
How reassuring is it to know that by methodically analyzing and addressing performance issues, you can significantly

boost the efficiency and reliability of an industrial process? These case studies highlight the transformative impact of diligent debugging and testing.

---

7. Continuous Improvement and Future Trends

The processes of debugging, testing, and troubleshooting are not one-time tasks but part of a continuous cycle of improvement. As systems evolve, new challenges will arise, and the methods for ensuring quality must also advance.

7.1 Embracing a Culture of Continuous Improvement

Key Strategies:

- **Regular Code Reviews:**
  Peer reviews help catch potential issues before they escalate.

- **Automated Testing Pipelines:**
  Continuous integration systems ensure that every code change is tested thoroughly.

- **User Feedback Loops:**
  Direct feedback from end-users provides invaluable insights into real-world performance.

- **Adaptive Monitoring:**
  Implement systems that automatically detect and alert you to anomalies in performance.

Actionable Steps:

1. **Establish Regular Review Cycles:**

   o Schedule periodic code reviews and testing sessions.

2. **Invest in Automation:**

   o Integrate CI/CD pipelines to automate tests and deployments.

3. **Collect and Analyze Feedback:**

   o Use analytics to track performance metrics and user satisfaction.

4. **Iterate:**

   o Continuously refine your processes and update your tools based on emerging best practices.

7.2 Future Trends in Debugging and Testing

Emerging Technologies:

- **AI-Powered Debugging Tools:**
  Future tools may leverage machine learning to predict bugs and suggest fixes automatically.

- **Advanced Monitoring Systems:**
  Real-time dashboards with predictive analytics will help prevent issues before they occur.

- **Virtual Reality (VR) for Debugging:**
  Immersive environments that allow developers to visualize and interact with their code in 3D could revolutionize debugging.

- **Cloud-Based Testing Platforms:**
  More scalable and collaborative testing environments that integrate seamlessly with development workflows.

Rhetorical Question:
Imagine a future where your debugging tools not only alert you to issues but also recommend fixes based on learned patterns. The future of testing and troubleshooting is bright, and you're on the cutting edge of this evolution.

---

8. Best Practices Recap: Your Debugging Toolkit

Let's summarize the best practices that will empower you to debug, test, and troubleshoot like a pro:

- **Systematic Approach:**
  Follow a structured process—reproduce, isolate, hypothesize, test, and fix.

- **Effective Use of Tools:**
  Leverage IDE debuggers, logging frameworks, profilers, and monitoring dashboards.

- **Automation:**
  Integrate automated tests into your development workflow to catch issues early.

- **Documentation:**
  Maintain comprehensive documentation and logs to track changes and troubleshoot effectively.

- **Peer Collaboration:**
  Engage in code reviews and collaborative debugging sessions to gain different perspectives.

- **Continuous Improvement:**
  Regularly update your testing and debugging practices to keep pace with new challenges and technologies.

Rhetorical Question:
Wouldn't it be amazing to have a robust toolkit that makes the process of troubleshooting almost second nature? With these best practices, you'll transform debugging from a dreaded task into a powerful pathway for innovation.

---

9. Final Words: Transforming Challenges into Opportunities

Debugging, testing, and troubleshooting are the cornerstones of successful development. Every error encountered is an opportunity to learn, improve, and build a more resilient system. As you refine your skills in these areas, you'll find that problems become puzzles waiting to be solved—a challenge that, once overcome, strengthens your entire project.

9.1 Embrace the Iterative Process

Remember, debugging and testing are not one-time events. They are part of an ongoing cycle that continually refines your system:

- **Iterate Frequently:**
  Make small, incremental changes and test often.

- **Celebrate Small Wins:**
  Each bug fixed and test passed is a step towards a more robust system.

- **Learn and Document:**
  Keep track of lessons learned to avoid repeating mistakes in the future.

9.2 The Future is Resilient

In a world where technology is advancing at breakneck speed, the ability to quickly identify and fix issues is invaluable. The principles and strategies outlined in this chapter will not only help you build reliable systems today but will also serve as a foundation for the resilient, adaptive technologies of tomorrow.

Rhetorical Question:

Are you ready to turn every challenge in your code into a stepping stone for success? With a disciplined approach to debugging, testing, and troubleshooting, you're well-equipped to lead your projects to excellence.

---

10. Conclusion: Mastering the Art of Debugging and Testing

In this chapter, we've explored the essential practices of debugging, testing, and troubleshooting. We've covered:

- **A Systematic Debugging Approach:**
  Reproducing, isolating, hypothesizing, testing, and fixing.

- **Diverse Testing Methodologies:**
  Unit, integration, system, and acceptance testing, all aimed at ensuring your code meets its intended goals.

- **Troubleshooting Strategies:**
  A structured process to identify root causes and implement effective solutions.

- **Best Practices and Tools:**
  The habits and technologies that make debugging and testing efficient and effective.

- **Real-World Case Studies:**
  Examples from autonomous vehicles, industrial

robotics, and more, illustrating how these practices lead to robust systems.

- **Continuous Improvement:**
  Embracing an iterative process that turns every challenge into an opportunity for growth.

As you continue your journey in technology and robotics, remember that the road to excellence is paved with well-tested, thoroughly debugged code. Every bug resolved and every test passed is a testament to your commitment to quality and innovation.

Rhetorical Question:
Are you ready to transform the challenges in your code into powerful opportunities for improvement? With the strategies and insights from this chapter, you're equipped to create systems that are not only functional but also resilient and robust.

11. Final Reflective Thought

Debugging, testing, and troubleshooting are more than just technical processes—they are an integral part of the creative journey in building technology. Like an artist refining their masterpiece, every fix and every test improves the final product, making it more beautiful, reliable, and impactful. Embrace these processes as opportunities to learn, iterate, and ultimately excel in your craft.

Rhetorical Question:

Will you let every challenge in your code be a lesson that propels you towards perfection, or will you see it as a roadblock? The choice is yours, and with the right mindset and tools, nothing can stop you from building the future.

Happy debugging, testing, and troubleshooting—your journey to crafting flawless systems starts now!

Chapter 11: Exploring Future Trends in Robotics

Welcome to a glimpse into tomorrow—a deep dive into the future trends shaping the robotics landscape. As technology accelerates, robotics continues to evolve, transforming industries, enhancing everyday life, and pushing the boundaries of what machines can achieve. In this chapter, we'll explore emerging technologies, innovative paradigms, and visionary concepts that promise to revolutionize robotics in the coming years. We'll break down complex ideas into clear, actionable steps, pepper the discussion with relatable analogies and rhetorical questions, and include visual aids to help you navigate these exciting trends. Whether you're an industry veteran or a curious newcomer, this guide will equip you with a forward-looking perspective on the dynamic world of robotics.

---

1. Introduction: A Glimpse Into Tomorrow

Imagine a world where robots not only perform mundane tasks but also learn, collaborate, and even anticipate human needs. This is not science fiction—it's the future that robotics is rapidly approaching. Today's robots are evolving from simple, pre-programmed machines to intelligent systems capable of adapting to complex environments and interacting seamlessly with humans.

1.1 The Evolution of Robotics

In recent decades, robotics has shifted from rigid industrial automation to flexible, adaptive systems that can work in dynamic, unstructured environments. This evolution is driven by advances in artificial intelligence, sensor technology, and connectivity. The future trends in robotics are not just incremental improvements; they represent paradigm shifts that will redefine how we live and work.

Key Drivers of Future Robotics:

- **Artificial Intelligence (AI) and Machine Learning:**
  Enabling robots to learn from data, make decisions, and improve over time.

- **Advanced Sensor Technologies:**
  Providing robots with a richer understanding of their surroundings.

- **Connectivity and Edge Computing:**
  Allowing real-time data processing and communication across distributed networks.

- **Collaborative and Swarm Robotics:**
  Where multiple robots work together seamlessly, each complementing the others' capabilities.

- **Human-Robot Interaction (HRI):**
  Fostering more natural, intuitive interactions between humans and machines.

Rhetorical Question:

Can you imagine a future where robots are as adaptive and intelligent as living beings, capable of learning from their environment and evolving to meet our needs? That's the exciting reality we're about to explore.

The Future Robotics Ecosystem

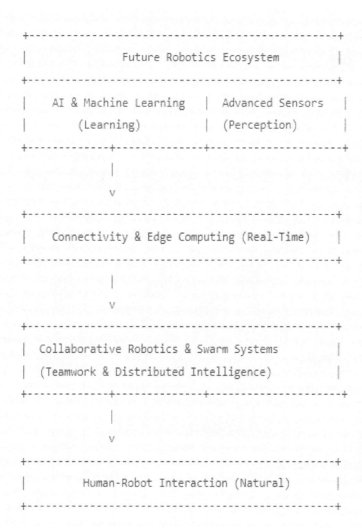

This diagram provides a high-level overview of the key components driving future robotics, illustrating how they interconnect to create a cohesive, intelligent ecosystem.

2. Emerging Technologies in Robotics

The landscape of robotics is being reshaped by breakthrough technologies that are setting the stage for next-generation innovations. In this section, we'll explore several of these technologies and explain how they're contributing to the evolution of robotics.

2.1 Artificial Intelligence and Machine Learning

What It Means:
AI and machine learning (ML) allow robots to process vast amounts of data, learn from their experiences, and make decisions autonomously. Unlike traditional programming, where every decision is hard-coded, ML models adapt and improve over time.

Step-by-Step Approach to Integrating AI:

1. **Data Collection:**
   - Gather data from sensors, cameras, and user interactions.
   - *Example:* A robot collects images and sensor data as it navigates a room.

2. **Data Preprocessing:**
   - Clean and organize the data to ensure consistency.
   - *Tip:* Normalize data to a standard scale.

3. **Model Selection and Training:**

- ○ Choose a machine learning model (e.g., convolutional neural networks for image recognition).

- ○ Train the model on your dataset using platforms like TensorFlow or PyTorch.

4. **Integration:**

- ○ Embed the trained model into your robot's decision-making module.

- ○ *Example:* Use the model to recognize obstacles and adjust the robot's path.

5. **Continuous Learning:**

- ○ Set up a feedback loop to update the model with new data over time.

- ○ *Tip:* Use online learning techniques for real-time improvements.

Rhetorical Question:
Wouldn't it be incredible if your robot could learn from every interaction, constantly becoming more efficient and smarter? That's the transformative power of AI in robotics.

3. The Rise of Collaborative and Swarm Robotics

Imagine a flock of birds moving in perfect harmony, each bird adjusting its flight based on its neighbors. This is the essence of collaborative and swarm robotics—where multiple robots operate as a cohesive unit, each one contributing to a larger mission. Collaborative robotics involves teamwork among machines, while swarm robotics focuses on the behavior of large numbers of simple robots working together.

3.1 Understanding Collaborative Robotics

Key Concepts:

- **Inter-Robot Communication:**
  Robots share information about their position, status, and environment.

- **Task Distribution:**
  Tasks are divided among robots based on their capabilities.

- **Decentralized Control:**
  Each robot makes decisions locally while contributing to a global objective.

Step-by-Step Approach to Building Collaborative Systems:

1. **Define the Collective Goal:**

- o Establish a clear mission that requires collaboration.

- o *Example:* A fleet of robots mapping an unknown environment.

2. **Develop Communication Protocols:**

   - o Use middleware like ROS2 to enable seamless communication.

   - o *Tip:* Implement topics and services for message passing.

3. **Implement Task Allocation:**

   - o Create algorithms to distribute tasks based on robot capabilities.

   - o *Example:* One robot scouts ahead while others follow to map detailed areas.

4. **Test Decentralized Control:**

   - o Simulate scenarios to ensure that local decision-making leads to effective global behavior.

5. **Iterate and Optimize:**

   - o Use feedback from simulations and real-world tests to refine coordination strategies.

Rhetorical Question:

Can you envision a team of robots that, like a well-rehearsed sports team, passes the baton flawlessly and adapts on the fly to overcome challenges? That's the promise of collaborative robotics.

Collaborative Robotics Architecture

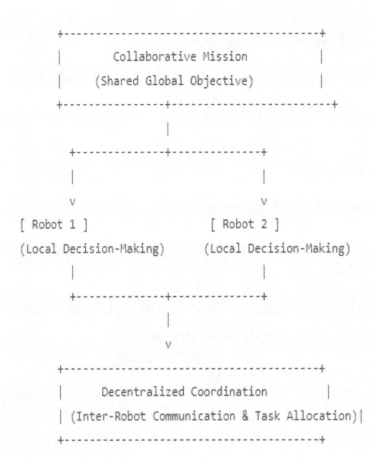

This diagram shows how individual robots contribute to a collective mission through decentralized decision-making and inter-robot communication.

3.2 Swarm Robotics: The Power of Numbers

Swarm robotics takes collaboration to an even larger scale, with potentially hundreds or thousands of simple robots operating together. This approach is inspired by nature—like ants building a colony or bees performing a hive dance.

Step-by-Step Approach to Swarm Robotics:

1. ### Define Simple Behavioral Rules:

   - Each robot follows basic rules that govern movement, obstacle avoidance, and communication.

2. ### Simulate Emergent Behavior:

   - Use simulations to observe how simple rules can lead to complex, collective behavior.

3. ### Deploy in Real-World Scenarios:

   - Start with small groups and scale up gradually.

4. ### Monitor and Optimize:

   - Continuously collect data to refine the rules and improve efficiency.

5. ### Leverage Redundancy:

   - Design the system so that the failure of individual robots doesn't compromise the overall mission.

Rhetorical Question:
Imagine a swarm of tiny robots that can cover a vast area to search for survivors in a disaster zone, each one playing a critical part in the mission. Isn't that a powerful vision for the future of robotics?

4. Human-Robot Interaction: Beyond the Interface

The future of robotics isn't just about machines operating in isolation—it's about creating systems that interact naturally with humans. Human-Robot Interaction (HRI) focuses on making these interactions as intuitive and seamless as possible.

4.1 The Evolution of HRI

Today's interfaces are evolving from clunky command-line inputs and rigid touchscreens to natural language processing, gesture recognition, and even emotional intelligence. Imagine a robot that can understand your tone of voice and adjust its behavior accordingly, or one that responds to your gestures without needing a manual prompt.

Step-by-Step Approach to Enhancing HRI:

1. **Identify Interaction Modalities:**

   o Choose input methods such as voice, touch, and gesture.

2. **Develop Natural Language Processing Capabilities:**

   o Use NLP libraries (e.g., spaCy, NLTK) to interpret user commands.

3. **Integrate Visual and Auditory Feedback:**

- o Design intuitive graphical interfaces and use text-to-speech for responses.

4. **Test with Real Users:**

- o Gather feedback to refine the interaction experience.

5. **Iterate and Personalize:**

- o Adapt the system based on individual user preferences and contexts.

Rhetorical Question:
Wouldn't it be transformative if interacting with a robot felt as natural as conversing with a friend? The future of HRI promises exactly that.

4.2 Real-World Example: Social Companion Robots

Scenario:
A social companion robot deployed in eldercare facilities interacts with residents through natural language and gestures, offering reminders, entertainment, and companionship.

Implementation Details:

1. **Input Methods:**

- o Voice recognition to capture commands and sentiments.

2. **Processing:**

- o NLP algorithms to understand requests and context.

3. **Output:**

- o A combination of visual displays and synthesized speech.

4. **Results:**

- o Improved resident engagement, enhanced mood, and a reduced sense of isolation.

5. **Iteration:**

- o Continuous refinement based on feedback from both users and caregivers.

Rhetorical Question:

Can you imagine a robot that not only helps with daily tasks but also provides genuine emotional support, transforming the lives of those in care? That's the future of human-robot interaction.

---

5. Robotics in Unconventional Environments

Robotics is expanding beyond traditional settings, venturing into environments that were once thought too challenging for machines. From deep underwater exploration to extreme space missions, robotics is redefining what's possible.

5.1 Underwater Robotics

Overview:
Underwater robots (or autonomous underwater vehicles, AUVs) are designed to operate in the depths of oceans, performing tasks such as environmental monitoring, pipeline inspection, and marine research.

Step-by-Step Approach:

1. **Define Mission Objectives:**

   o   Determine the task (e.g., coral reef mapping, search for underwater cables).

2. **Design a Robust Platform:**

   o   Ensure the robot is waterproof and pressure-resistant.

3. **Integrate Specialized Sensors:**

   o   Use sonar, depth sensors, and underwater cameras.

4. **Develop Navigation Algorithms:**

   o   Adapt SLAM techniques to the underwater environment.

5. **Test in Controlled Conditions:**

   o   Use simulation tanks and shallow water tests before deep-sea deployment.

Rhetorical Question:

Imagine a robot that can explore the mysterious depths of the ocean, uncovering secrets hidden for millennia—what wonders might it reveal?

5.2 Space Robotics

Overview:

Space robotics is a field dedicated to exploring extraterrestrial environments, repairing satellites, and even constructing structures in orbit. Robots like Mars rovers and robotic arms on the International Space Station (ISS) exemplify these advancements.

Step-by-Step Approach:

1. **Define the Space Mission:**

    ○ Outline objectives such as planetary exploration or satellite servicing.

2. **Design for Extremes:**

    ○ Build systems that can withstand radiation, extreme temperatures, and microgravity.

3. **Integrate Advanced Sensors:**

    ○ Use cameras, spectrometers, and environmental sensors.

4. **Implement Autonomous Navigation:**

    ○ Develop algorithms that allow robots to navigate unstructured, alien terrain.

5. **Test with Simulations:**

  - Use high-fidelity simulators to mimic space conditions before deployment.

Rhetorical Question:
What mysteries of the cosmos could be unraveled if robots could venture where humans cannot? The next generation of space robotics promises to expand our horizons like never before.

5.3 Robotics in Hazardous Environments

Overview:
Robots are increasingly used in hazardous environments—nuclear plants, disaster zones, and chemical spills—to perform tasks that would endanger human lives.

Step-by-Step Approach:

1. **Identify the Hazard:**

  - Understand the environment and the specific risks involved.

2. **Design a Safe, Robust System:**

  - Choose materials and components that can resist the hazard (e.g., radiation-hardened circuits).

3. **Integrate Redundant Safety Features:**

  - Build in fail-safes and emergency stop mechanisms.

4. **Develop Remote Control Capabilities:**

   o Ensure operators can control the robot from a
   safe distance.

5. **Conduct Rigorous Field Testing:**

   o Test in simulated hazardous environments to
   validate performance.

Rhetorical Question:
How reassuring is it to know that robots can step into danger
for us, protecting human lives while ensuring that critical
tasks are completed safely? The future of robotics in
hazardous environments is not just about technology—it's
about safeguarding our future.

6. Ethical and Societal Implications of Future Robotics

As robotics technology advances, it brings profound ethical
and societal considerations. Future robotics will not only
change how we work but also how we live, raising questions
about privacy, employment, safety, and even human identity.

6.1 Key Ethical Considerations

1. **Privacy and Data Security:**

   • **Definition:**
   Ensuring that robots collecting data do so responsibly
   and that sensitive information is protected.

- **Actionable Steps:**

  1. Implement strong encryption protocols.

  2. Establish clear data governance policies.

  3. Regularly audit systems for vulnerabilities.

2. Employment and Workforce Impact:

- **Definition:**
  Understanding how automation affects jobs and developing strategies for workforce transition.

- **Actionable Steps:**

  1. Engage stakeholders to assess impact.

  2. Develop retraining programs.

  3. Promote policies that balance innovation with social responsibility.

3. Safety and Accountability:

- **Definition:**
  Ensuring that robots operate safely in human environments and that accountability is clearly defined in case of failures.

- **Actionable Steps:**

  1. Implement rigorous safety standards.

  2. Define clear lines of accountability.

  3. Use fail-safe mechanisms and redundancy.

Rhetorical Question:

How can we ensure that as robots become more integrated into our lives, they do so in a manner that respects our privacy, protects our jobs, and keeps us safe? These ethical considerations are as crucial as the technology itself.

6.2 Societal Impact and Policy Development

Actionable Steps for Policymakers and Industry Leaders:

1. **Stakeholder Engagement:**

   o Collaborate with communities, industry experts, and ethicists.

2. **Develop Regulatory Frameworks:**

   o Establish standards that guide the ethical development and deployment of robotics.

3. **Public Awareness and Education:**

   o Inform the public about the benefits and risks of advanced robotics.

4. **Long-Term Impact Studies:**

   o Fund research to study the societal effects of robotics over time.

Rhetorical Question:

Wouldn't it be wise to shape a future where the benefits of robotics are shared by all, and where technological progress is balanced by ethical responsibility? Societal impact and policy are key to achieving that vision.

7. Preparing for the Future: How to Stay Ahead in Robotics

The rapid evolution of robotics technology means that staying current is a continuous process. Whether you're a researcher, developer, or entrepreneur, preparing for the future requires a proactive and adaptive mindset.

7.1 Lifelong Learning and Skill Development

Actionable Steps:

1. **Pursue Continuous Education:**

   o Enroll in courses, attend workshops, and participate in webinars on emerging robotics technologies.

   o *Example:* Online platforms like Coursera and edX offer specialized courses in AI, machine learning, and robotics.

2. **Participate in Professional Communities:**

   o Join robotics forums, attend industry conferences, and collaborate with peers.

   o *Tip:* Engage in hackathons and local meetups to gain hands-on experience.

3. **Experiment with New Technologies:**

- ○ Regularly test and implement emerging tools and methodologies.

- ○ *Example:* Experiment with edge computing solutions or cloud-based robotics platforms.

7.2 Adopting a Future-Proof Mindset

Key Principles:

- **Flexibility:**
  Design systems that can adapt to new technologies and changing requirements.

- **Scalability:**
  Ensure that your solutions can grow in scope and complexity.

- **Interdisciplinary Collaboration:**
  Work with experts from fields such as AI, cybersecurity, and human factors to create comprehensive solutions.

Step-by-Step Approach:

1. **Evaluate Current Skills:**

   - ○ Identify areas where you need improvement.

2. **Set Learning Goals:**

   - ○ Define clear, measurable objectives for skill development.

3. **Implement a Continuous Improvement Plan:**

- o Regularly review and update your knowledge base.

4. **Adopt New Tools and Technologies:**

   - o Stay abreast of industry trends and integrate new methods into your workflow.

Rhetorical Question:
Are you ready to embrace a mindset of continuous learning and adaptability, ensuring that your skills and solutions remain at the cutting edge of robotics? The future belongs to those who never stop learning.

---

8. The Role of Industry and Academia in Shaping the Future

The future of robotics is not built by individuals alone—it's a collaborative effort between industry, academia, and governments. Together, these entities are driving innovation, setting standards, and creating the next generation of robotics technologies.

8.1 Industry-Academia Collaborations

Key Strategies:

- **Joint Research Initiatives:**
   - o Collaborative projects that combine academic research with practical industry applications.

- **Internship and Fellowship Programs:**

  - Opportunities for students to gain hands-on experience in cutting-edge robotics research.

- **Conferences and Workshops:**

  - Platforms for sharing breakthroughs, networking, and setting future research agendas.

Actionable Steps:

1. **Identify Leading Institutions and Companies:**

   - Research which organizations are at the forefront of robotics innovation.

2. **Participate in Collaborative Projects:**

   - Engage in joint research initiatives, contribute to open-source projects, and attend industry conferences.

3. **Leverage Funding Opportunities:**

   - Apply for grants and scholarships dedicated to robotics research and development.

8.2 Government Policies and Standards

Key Areas of Focus:

- **Regulation and Compliance:**

  - Establishing standards that ensure the safety, privacy, and ethical use of robotics.

- **Investment in R&D:**

  o Government funding for research and development initiatives in robotics.

- **International Collaboration:**

  o Cooperative efforts across borders to set global standards and foster innovation.

Actionable Steps:

1. **Stay Informed on Policy Developments:**

   o Follow government announcements, regulatory changes, and industry guidelines.

2. **Advocate for Responsible Innovation:**

   o Engage with policymakers and contribute to public discourse on the future of robotics.

3. **Implement Best Practices in Your Work:**

   o Ensure your projects comply with current standards and are designed to be adaptable to future regulations.

Rhetorical Question:
How can a united effort between industry, academia, and government accelerate the development of robotics while ensuring that technology benefits society as a whole? Collaboration is the key to unlocking a prosperous future.

9. Future Scenarios: Envisioning Tomorrow's Robotics

Let's take a moment to imagine some future scenarios that encapsulate the trends we've discussed. These scenarios are not predictions but inspirations—visions of what might be possible as robotics continues to evolve.

9.1 Scenario 1: The Smart, Autonomous City

Imagine:
A city where every component—traffic lights, public transportation, waste management, and emergency services—is connected through a network of intelligent robots. These robots communicate in real time, optimizing traffic flow, coordinating rapid responses to emergencies, and maintaining infrastructure with minimal human intervention.

Key Features:

- Autonomous delivery drones ensure timely delivery of goods.

- Robotic maintenance crews monitor and repair infrastructure.

- Emergency response robots collaborate with human first responders.

- A centralized AI system oversees city operations, adapting to changing conditions dynamically.

Step-by-Step Vision:

1. **Infrastructure Integration:**

   o Implement city-wide sensors and communication networks.

2. **Deploy Robotic Fleets:**

   o Introduce specialized robots for transportation, maintenance, and emergency response.

3. **Central Coordination:**

   o Use AI to manage and optimize operations across the entire city.

4. **Public Engagement:**

   o Develop user-friendly interfaces for residents to interact with the system.

Rhetorical Question:

Can you imagine living in a city where everything works in perfect harmony, where technology not only makes life easier but also enhances community well-being? That's the promise of a smart, autonomous city.

Smart City Robotics Ecosystem

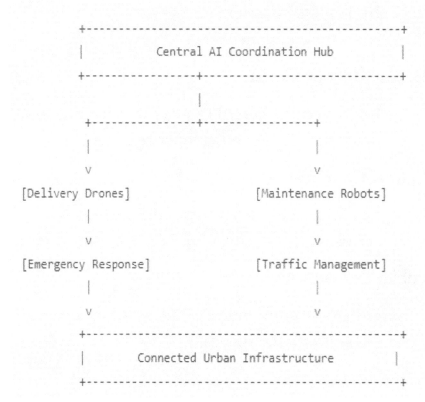

This diagram visualizes the interconnected components of a smart city, showcasing how various robotic systems work together under centralized coordination.

9.2 Scenario 2: Personalized Healthcare Robotics

Imagine:

Hospitals and homes equipped with personalized healthcare robots that not only assist with daily activities but also monitor health parameters in real time, alerting caregivers at the first sign of trouble. These robots offer companionship, deliver medications, and even perform routine diagnostic tests.

Key Features:

- Wearable sensors and home-based robots track vital signs continuously.

- AI-driven diagnostics provide early warnings for potential health issues.

- Interactive interfaces enable seamless communication between patients, robots, and healthcare providers.

- Personalized care plans adapt over time based on real-time data and patient feedback.

Step-by-Step Vision:

1. **Integrate Wearable and Home Sensors:**

   o Deploy devices that capture vital health data.

2. **Develop a Centralized Health Monitoring System:**

   o Use AI to analyze data and generate alerts.

3. **Implement Interactive Care Robots:**

   o Equip robots with NLP and facial recognition for personalized interaction.

4. **Facilitate Remote Consultations:**

   o Connect robots to healthcare providers for continuous monitoring and consultation.

Rhetorical Question:

What if a robot could be your personal health assistant, always on the lookout for any sign of trouble and ready to help at a moment's notice? Personalized healthcare robotics promises a future where medical care is proactive, personalized, and accessible.

9.3 Scenario 3: Space Exploration and Colonization

Imagine:

Robotic systems that pave the way for human colonization of Mars and beyond. Autonomous rovers, construction robots, and habitat maintenance systems work together in harsh extraterrestrial environments, building the infrastructure needed for long-term human settlement.

Key Features:

- Autonomous rovers map the Martian surface and identify resource-rich areas.

- Construction robots assemble habitats using local materials.

- Collaborative systems maintain life-support and communication networks.

- AI systems continuously adapt to the unpredictable space environment.

Step-by-Step Vision:

1. **Deploy Autonomous Rovers:**

   o Map the terrain and assess environmental conditions.

2. **Initiate Construction Operations:**

   o Use robots to build initial habitats and infrastructure.

3. **Establish Continuous Monitoring:**

   o Implement sensor networks and AI to monitor habitat conditions.

4. **Develop Interplanetary Communication:**

   o Ensure reliable data exchange between Earth and Mars.

5. **Foster Human-Robot Collaboration:**

   o Train robots to work alongside human settlers, providing support and maintenance.

Rhetorical Question:
Can you envision the thrill of exploring new worlds with a robotic crew that prepares the way for human settlers, making space colonization a reality? The future of space exploration is filled with boundless potential.

10. Conclusion: Embracing the Future of Robotics

As we've journeyed through these future scenarios, it becomes clear that the robotics landscape is on the brink of a revolutionary transformation. The trends and technologies discussed here are not just possibilities—they are actively shaping the future across diverse fields, from smart cities and personalized healthcare to space exploration and beyond.

10.1 Key Takeaways

- **Innovation is Constant:**
  Future robotics is driven by rapid advancements in AI, sensor technology, connectivity, and collaborative systems.

- **Interdisciplinary Collaboration:**
  The convergence of robotics with fields like healthcare, urban planning, and space science is creating integrated systems that improve lives.

- **Proactive Adaptation:**
  Staying ahead in robotics requires a mindset of continuous learning, adaptability, and a commitment to ethical innovation.

- **Real-World Impact:**
  From enhancing efficiency in manufacturing to saving lives in disaster zones, the future of robotics promises tangible benefits across all sectors.

10.2 Your Role in Shaping the Future

Every one of us—whether as researchers, developers, entrepreneurs, or enthusiasts—plays a part in this evolving story. The future trends in robotics present opportunities to create systems that are not only more capable and efficient but also more human-centric, ethical, and sustainable.

Rhetorical Question:
Are you ready to embrace these future trends and contribute to a world where robots work hand in hand with humans, driving progress and improving our quality of life?

---

11. Final Reflective Thought

Exploring future trends in robotics is more than a technical journey—it's an invitation to reimagine the world we live in. Each innovation, from intelligent AI systems to collaborative swarm robotics, is a building block for a future where technology and humanity are seamlessly intertwined. These trends promise to make our cities smarter, our healthcare more responsive, and our exploration of the universe even more daring.

As you continue your journey in robotics, ask yourself: How can I contribute to this future? How can my work help shape a world where technology is harnessed for the greater good, where robots not only perform tasks but also enhance our human experience?

Rhetorical Question:
Are you ready to be a part of the revolution that transforms challenges into opportunities, pushing the boundaries of what's possible and creating a future where robotics makes a meaningful difference in every facet of life?

---

12. Resources and Next Steps

To further your understanding and keep up with the rapidly evolving field of robotics, consider the following resources and actionable steps:

Books and Publications

- **"The Singularity Is Near" by Ray Kurzweil:**
  A visionary look at the future of technology and robotics.

- **"Robotics: Modelling, Planning and Control" by Bruno Siciliano and Lorenzo Sciavicco:**
  A comprehensive guide to advanced robotics concepts.

- **"Artificial Intelligence for Robotics" by Francis X. Govers:**
  Focused on integrating AI with robotics for intelligent systems.

Online Courses and Webinars

- **Coursera, edX, and Udacity:**
  Explore courses on AI, robotics, and machine learning.

- **MIT OpenCourseWare:**
  Access free, high-quality courses on robotics and control systems.

- **Industry Webinars:**
  Stay updated with webinars hosted by robotics companies and research institutions.

Tools and Software

- **ROS2 (Robot Operating System):**
  A critical middleware for multi-robot and collaborative systems.

- **Gazebo and RViz:**
  Simulation and visualization tools to test and refine your designs.

- **TensorFlow and PyTorch:**
  Essential for developing AI models that drive future robotics applications.

Communities and Conferences

- **IEEE Robotics and Automation Society:**
  Engage with a global community of professionals.

- **IROS (Intelligent Robots and Systems) and ICRA (International Conference on Robotics and Automation):**

Attend conferences to learn about the latest research and trends.

- **Local Robotics Meetups and Hackathons:** Network, share ideas, and collaborate on innovative projects.

Actionable Next Steps

1. **Set Learning Goals:**

   - Identify areas where you want to deepen your expertise (e.g., AI integration, swarm robotics, HRI).

2. **Build a Portfolio Project:**

   - Create a prototype that incorporates some of the future trends discussed here.

3. **Engage with the Community:**

   - Join online forums, attend meetups, and collaborate with peers to share knowledge.

4. **Stay Informed:**

   - Regularly read industry publications, follow thought leaders, and participate in webinars.

5. **Experiment and Innovate:**

   - Allocate time for R&D, experiment with new tools, and iterate on your designs continuously.

Rhetorical Question:
Wouldn't it be empowering to have a clear roadmap for staying ahead in the rapidly evolving world of robotics? With the right resources and a proactive mindset, you can be at the forefront of innovation.

---

13. Conclusion: The Future is in Your Hands

As we conclude our exploration of future trends in robotics, one thing becomes abundantly clear: the future is not something that happens to us; it's something we create. The trends and technologies we've discussed—from AI and collaborative robotics to advanced human-robot interaction and space exploration—are not distant dreams but emerging realities.

By embracing these trends, investing in continuous learning, and fostering collaboration between industry, academia, and governments, you have the opportunity to shape a world where robotics makes life better for everyone. Whether you're designing smart cities, enhancing healthcare, or exploring the cosmos, the innovations of tomorrow are being built today.

Final Reflective Thought:
Imagine a future where every challenge is met with a robotic solution—where machines learn, adapt, and collaborate to create a safer, more efficient, and more connected world.

This future is yours to shape. With every breakthrough, every prototype, and every collaborative project, you are contributing to the evolution of technology.

Rhetorical Question:

Are you ready to be a pioneer in this exciting new era of robotics? The journey ahead is full of challenges, opportunities, and endless possibilities. Embrace the future with confidence, and let your innovations light the way for generations to come.

Happy exploring, and may your journey in robotics be as limitless as your imagination!

Chapter 12: Conclusion and Next Steps

Welcome to the final chapter—a reflective journey that ties together all you've learned and paves the way for your future in robotics and technology. In this chapter, we'll summarize key insights, share actionable next steps, and inspire you to continue innovating. Whether you're an industry professional, a hobbyist, or a curious learner, this guide will equip you with a clear roadmap for moving forward. We'll break down each idea into clear, actionable steps, use relatable analogies to illustrate concepts, and provide visual aids to cement your understanding. Let's embark on this concluding journey together, ensuring that every challenge becomes an opportunity and every next step a leap toward innovation.

1. Reflecting on the Journey: Key Takeaways

Before we look forward, it's crucial to reflect on the transformative journey you've undertaken. Throughout this guide, you've explored foundational and advanced robotics concepts, learned to build simulations and intelligent systems, and discovered real-world applications that are reshaping industries. Now, let's encapsulate those learnings into actionable insights.

1.1 Summary of Major Lessons

Key Lessons:

1. **Foundational Understanding:**

   o Grasped the basics of robotics architecture, including ROS2 fundamentals, sensor integration, and control algorithms.

2. **Advanced Techniques:**

   o Explored SLAM, AI integration, multi-robot coordination, and human-robot interaction.

3. **Practical Implementation:**

   o Built simulations, developed prototypes, and studied real-world applications—from manufacturing to healthcare and beyond.

4. **Problem-Solving Mindset:**

   o Emphasized systematic debugging, rigorous testing, and continuous troubleshooting as cornerstones of reliable systems.

5. **Future Trends and Innovation:**

   o Envisioned future robotics landscapes, including smart cities, swarm robotics, and space exploration, highlighting the ever-evolving nature of the field.

Relatable Analogy:

Think of your journey as constructing a skyscraper. You started with a solid foundation, built floors one by one, and added cutting-edge technology as you ascended. Now, as you reach the top, you not only admire the structure you've built but also envision the limitless skyline that awaits.

---

2. Setting the Stage for the Future: Your Next Steps

As we turn our gaze to the future, it's time to chart a clear path for your continued growth and innovation in robotics. The next steps you take will be crucial in transforming your knowledge into impactful projects and groundbreaking solutions.

2.1 Define Your Personal Goals

Step-by-Step Approach:

1. **Identify Your Passion Areas:**

   - What aspects of robotics excite you the most? Is it autonomous vehicles, healthcare, space exploration, or something else?

2. **Set Clear Objectives:**

   - Write down specific, measurable goals. *Example:* "I want to build a prototype for an autonomous drone delivery system within the next 12 months."

3. **Break Down Goals:**

  o Divide your main goal into smaller, manageable tasks.
  Example:

   • Research drone navigation systems.

   • Develop a simulation environment.

   • Build a basic prototype.

4. **Create a Timeline:**

  o Assign deadlines to each task to keep yourself accountable.

Actionable Tip:
Write your goals in a journal or create a digital roadmap. Regularly revisit and update your progress.

3. Building on Your Knowledge: Continuing Education and Skill Development

The field of robotics is dynamic, and continuous learning is essential to stay ahead. Embracing lifelong learning not only enhances your skills but also keeps you informed about the latest trends and technologies.

3.1 Strategies for Continuous Learning

Step-by-Step Approach:

1. **Enroll in Advanced Courses:**

   o Identify online platforms like Coursera, edX, and Udacity that offer courses in AI, robotics, and machine learning.

2. **Attend Workshops and Conferences:**

   o Participate in industry events such as ICRA, IROS, and IEEE conferences to network and learn from experts.

3. **Join Professional Communities:**

   o Engage with online forums, local meetups, and robotics clubs to share ideas and collaborate.

4. **Read Industry Publications:**

   o Subscribe to journals, blogs, and newsletters that cover the latest robotics innovations.

5. **Experiment with Projects:**

   o Apply new knowledge by building small projects or prototypes.

Actionable Tip:
Set aside dedicated time each week for learning—whether it's reading articles, watching tutorials, or working on a side project.

4. Collaborating and Networking: Building a Community

In robotics, collaboration is the engine of innovation. Networking with peers, mentors, and industry leaders not only broadens your perspective but also opens doors to new opportunities and collaborations.

4.1 How to Build and Leverage Your Network

Step-by-Step Approach:

1. **Identify Relevant Communities:**

   o Look for online forums, LinkedIn groups, and local robotics clubs.

2. **Attend Meetups and Conferences:**

   o Engage with professionals at industry events.

3. **Share Your Work:**

   o Publish your projects on GitHub or personal blogs to showcase your skills.

4. **Seek Mentorship:**

   o Connect with experienced professionals who can provide guidance and feedback.

5. **Collaborate on Projects:**

- o Join collaborative projects or hackathons to gain practical experience and broaden your network.

Actionable Tip:

Regularly participate in discussions, offer help to others, and be open to collaboration. The more you give, the more you receive.

5. Transitioning from Learning to Implementation: Building Your Next Big Project

The ultimate goal of all learning is to put knowledge into action. Whether you're an entrepreneur, a researcher, or a hobbyist, the next step is to apply your skills to build innovative projects that solve real-world problems.

5.1 Planning Your Next Project

Step-by-Step Approach:

1. **Identify a Problem or Opportunity:**

   - o Look for gaps in the market or challenges in your community that robotics can solve.

   - o *Example:* "Develop a service robot to assist elderly residents with daily tasks."

2. **Define Your Project Scope:**

- o Outline the project's objectives, requirements, and expected outcomes.
- o Use a project planning tool or create a simple flowchart.

3. **Assemble a Team:**

- o If applicable, collaborate with peers who have complementary skills.
- o Clearly define roles and responsibilities.

4. **Develop a Prototype:**

- o Start with a minimum viable product (MVP) to test key functionalities.
- o Iterate based on feedback and testing.

5. **Test and Validate:**

- o Rigorously test the prototype in controlled and real-world scenarios.
- o Gather user feedback and make improvements.

6. **Scale and Deploy:**

- o Once validated, plan for scaling your solution.
- o Consider production, marketing, and long-term maintenance.

Actionable Tip:
Document every step of your project, from planning to

deployment. This not only helps in troubleshooting but also serves as a valuable portfolio piece.

---

6. Integrating Emerging Trends into Your Projects

As you plan and build your projects, it's crucial to integrate emerging trends in robotics to keep your solutions innovative and competitive. Let's explore how to adopt these trends in a practical, step-by-step manner.

6.1 Identifying Relevant Trends

Step-by-Step Approach:

1. **Research Current Innovations:**

   o Read industry publications, attend webinars, and follow thought leaders.

   o *Example:* Follow journals on AI, sensor technology, and collaborative robotics.

2. **Assess Relevance to Your Project:**

   o Determine which trends could enhance your project's functionality or efficiency.

   o *Example:* Integrate edge computing for faster processing in autonomous systems.

3. **Prioritize Trends:**

- o Evaluate the potential impact and feasibility of each trend.

- o Create a short list of trends that align with your project goals.

6.2 Implementing Emerging Technologies

Actionable Steps:

1. **Prototype Integration:**

   - o Develop small prototypes or modules that incorporate new technologies.

   - o Test these modules separately before integrating them into your main project.

2. **Iterate and Optimize:**

   - o Use feedback from testing to refine the integration.

   - o Monitor performance metrics to ensure that the technology adds value.

3. **Document Learnings:**

   - o Keep detailed records of challenges and successes.

   - o This documentation will be invaluable for future projects and for sharing insights with the community.

7. Preparing for a Dynamic Future: Next Steps in Your Journey

The conclusion of this guide is not the end—it's the beginning of a new chapter in your robotics journey. Armed with the knowledge and tools from this guide, it's time to take decisive steps toward creating your future.

7.1 Immediate Next Steps

Actionable Steps:

1. **Review Your Learnings:**

   o Revisit key concepts and reflect on how they apply to your projects.

   o Create a summary document that highlights your most important takeaways.

2. **Set Short-Term Goals:**

   o Define immediate projects or tasks you want to complete in the next 3-6 months.

   o Use the SMART criteria (Specific, Measurable, Achievable, Relevant, Time-bound).

3. **Plan Long-Term Objectives:**

   o Envision where you want to be in 1-3 years.

   o Outline career or project milestones, such as developing a prototype or publishing a research paper.

4. **Engage in Networking:**

   - Reach out to mentors, join professional groups, and attend events.

   - Build relationships with peers who share your vision.

5. **Start a New Project:**

   - Apply what you've learned to a real-world problem.

   - Document your process and share your findings with the community.

---

8. Fostering Innovation: Embracing a Culture of Experimentation

Innovation thrives in environments where experimentation is encouraged and failure is seen as a stepping stone to success. In robotics, as in any creative field, the willingness to experiment, iterate, and learn from mistakes is paramount.

8.1 Cultivating a Mindset for Innovation

Step-by-Step Approach:

1. **Embrace Failure as Learning:**

   - Recognize that every failed experiment is a valuable lesson.

    o   Document what went wrong and why.

2. **Encourage Experimentation:**

    o   Set aside time and resources for research and development.

    o   Create small, low-risk projects to test new ideas.

3. **Iterate Quickly:**

    o   Use agile methodologies to implement changes rapidly.

    o   Regularly review and refine your projects based on feedback.

4. **Celebrate Innovations:**

    o   Recognize and reward breakthroughs, no matter how small.

    o   Share successes with your team or community to inspire further creativity.

Actionable Tip:
Create an "innovation journal" where you record experiments, ideas, and insights. Over time, this journal becomes a treasure trove of inspiration and lessons learned.

9. Final Reflective Thought: Your Legacy in Robotics

As you stand at the threshold of a new era in your robotics journey, take a moment to reflect on what you've achieved and the legacy you want to build. Every line of code, every project, and every innovation is a building block in the future of technology. Your work has the potential to shape industries, improve lives, and redefine the boundaries of what robots can do.

Reflective Questions:

- What problems do you feel most passionate about solving?

- How can your innovations contribute to a more connected, efficient, and humane world?

- In what ways can you inspire others to follow in your footsteps and push the boundaries of technology?

Relatable Analogy:
Consider your journey like a relay race where every innovation you pass on becomes a baton that others can carry forward. Your legacy in robotics is not just about what you build but also about how you inspire the next generation of innovators.

---

10. Conclusion: The Journey Ahead Is Bright

In this final chapter, we've reviewed your journey—from the foundational concepts of robotics to advanced applications and real-world case studies—and laid out a clear path for your next steps. The future of robotics is filled with promise, and you have the tools, knowledge, and mindset to be a part of that exciting evolution.

Key Points to Remember:

- **Reflect on Your Learnings:**
  Understand how each piece of knowledge builds a stronger, more innovative foundation.

- **Set Clear Goals:**
  Define both short-term projects and long-term aspirations.

- **Embrace Continuous Learning:**
  Stay informed, be curious, and always look for ways to improve.

- **Foster a Culture of Collaboration and Experimentation:**
  Engage with your community, share your insights, and never be afraid to try new ideas.

- **Prepare for a Dynamic Future:**
  Adapt to emerging trends and technologies to keep your projects relevant and impactful.

Rhetorical Question:
Are you ready to seize the future and transform challenges into opportunities, innovation into reality, and ideas into groundbreaking projects? The journey ahead is yours to define, and the possibilities are endless.

11. Action Plan: Your 30-60-90 Day Roadmap

To help you transition from learning to action, here's a practical 30-60-90 day plan that outlines what you can achieve in the near term.

11.1 The First 30 Days: Foundation Building

- **Week 1-2: Review and Reflect**
    - Re-read key sections of your learning materials.
    - Document your key takeaways and identify areas for improvement.

- **Week 3: Set Personal Goals**
    - Define one or two short-term projects you'd like to tackle.
    - Outline specific objectives and milestones.

- **Week 4: Join a Community**
    - Engage with online forums, attend a local meetup, or join a professional group.
    - Start building a network of peers and mentors.

Actionable Checklist:

- Summarize learnings in a dedicated journal.
- Define at least two project ideas with clear objectives.

- Sign up for at least one robotics forum or local meetup.

11.2 The Next 60 Days: Project Initiation and Skill Enhancement

- **Month 2: Prototype Development**
  - Begin developing your first prototype based on one of your project ideas.
  - Use simulation tools and prototyping platforms to test your ideas.

- **Skill Enhancement:**
  - Take an advanced online course in a niche area that interests you (e.g., AI integration, swarm robotics).
  - Participate in a hackathon or workshop.

- **Collaboration:**
  - Reach out to potential collaborators from your network to discuss your project.
  - Set up regular brainstorming sessions.

Actionable Checklist:

- Develop a prototype or proof-of-concept for one project.

- Enroll in an advanced robotics course.

- Organize a brainstorming session with peers.

11.3 The Next 90 Days: Refinement, Testing, and Scaling

- **Month 3: Refine and Test**

  - Rigorously test your prototype in various scenarios.

  - Gather feedback from users or mentors and iterate on your design.

- **Plan for Scaling:**

  - Begin planning how to transition your prototype into a larger, scalable project.

  - Consider the business, technical, and user experience aspects.

- **Share and Document:**

  - Publish your progress on platforms like GitHub or a personal blog.

  - Document your journey, challenges, and breakthroughs to share with the community.

Actionable Checklist:

- Refine your prototype based on testing and feedback.
- Develop a scaling plan for your project.

- Publish your work online and seek constructive feedback.

30-60-90 Day Roadmap

```
+-------------------------------+
|          First 30 Days        |
|    (Review, Set Goals, Join   |
|          Community)           |
+-------------+-----------------+
              |
              v
+-------------------------------+
|          Next 60 Days         |
|  (Prototype Development,       |
|    Skill Enhancement,         |
|    Collaboration)             |
+-------------+-----------------+
              |
              v
+-------------------------------+
|          Next 90 Days         |
|  (Refinement, Testing,        |
|    Scaling, Documentation)    |
+-------------------------------+
```

Explanation:

This diagram visually represents your 30-60-90 day action plan, providing a structured timeline to transition from learning to implementing and scaling your projects.

Rhetorical Question:
Are you ready to take the leap from theory to practice with a concrete, step-by-step plan that guides you over the next 90 days? Your roadmap to success starts now.

---

12. Final Reflections and Inspirational Words

As we close this final chapter, take a moment to reflect on your journey and the exciting road ahead. Robotics is not just about machines; it's about pushing boundaries, solving problems, and creating a future where technology serves humanity in profound ways.

12.1 Your Legacy in Robotics

Every project you build, every problem you solve, contributes to the broader narrative of innovation. Your work can inspire others, spark new ideas, and pave the way for the next generation of technological breakthroughs.

Inspirational Reminders:

- **Embrace Challenges:**
  Each obstacle is an opportunity to learn and grow.

- **Stay Curious:**
  The world of robotics is vast and ever-changing—never stop exploring.

- **Collaborate:**
  Innovation thrives in communities. Share your ideas
  and learn from others.

- **Be Resilient:**
  Persistence is the key to turning setbacks into stepping
  stones.

Rhetorical Question:
What kind of legacy do you want to leave in the world of
robotics? Imagine the impact of your work on future
generations—this is your chance to build a future where
technology empowers and uplifts us all.

---

13. Your Call to Action: Step into the Future

Now is the moment to transition from reflection to action.
The future of robotics is not a distant horizon; it's here,
waiting for innovators like you to shape it. Your journey has
equipped you with knowledge, skills, and a vision. All that's
left is to put it into action.

13.1 Immediate Actions You Can Take Today

- **Review Your Accomplishments:**
  Take a moment to review your portfolio, reflect on the
  projects you've completed, and celebrate your
  progress.

- **Set New Goals:**
  Write down your next project ideas, focusing on areas that ignite your passion.

- **Reach Out:**
  Contact mentors, join online forums, and start discussions with peers.

- **Experiment:**
  Tinker with a small project or prototype that incorporates a new trend or technology you're excited about.

- **Document Your Journey:**
  Start a blog or a journal detailing your progress, challenges, and breakthroughs.

13.2 Long-Term Vision

Think about where you want to be in the next five years. Envision a future where your projects have not only achieved technical success but have also made a positive impact on society. Whether it's developing cutting-edge healthcare robots, contributing to smart city initiatives, or pioneering space exploration, your long-term vision should be bold and inspiring.

Steps to Achieve Your Vision:

1. **Develop a Strategic Plan:**

   - Outline your long-term goals and the steps needed to achieve them.

2. **Invest in Continuous Learning:**

   o Stay updated with the latest trends and technologies.

3. **Build a Support Network:**

   o Surround yourself with mentors, collaborators, and peers who share your vision.

4. **Pursue Funding Opportunities:**

   o Look for grants, investments, or partnerships to support your ambitious projects.

5. **Measure and Adapt:**

   o Regularly review your progress, measure outcomes, and adjust your strategy accordingly.

14. Final Words: Your Future in Robotics Starts Now

As we bring this guide to a close, remember that the end of one chapter is just the beginning of another. Your journey in robotics is a continuous path of discovery, innovation, and impact. The skills and knowledge you've acquired here have prepared you to tackle the challenges of today and tomorrow with confidence and creativity.

Key Reminders:

- **Embrace the Process:**
  Debugging, testing, and troubleshooting are not setbacks but opportunities to refine and perfect your work.

- **Stay Curious:**
  Always seek out new knowledge, challenge the status quo, and never stop asking "what if?"

- **Collaborate and Innovate:**
  The power of robotics lies in collaboration—work with others, share your ideas, and build on collective wisdom.

- **Be Resilient:**
  Every obstacle is a chance to learn and improve. Your persistence and dedication will define your success.

Rhetorical Question:
Will you step boldly into the future, armed with the knowledge, passion, and determination to revolutionize robotics? The world of technology is waiting for your innovative spirit.

15. Conclusion: Your Future is Limitless

As you close this guide and look toward the horizon, know that the future of robotics is as limitless as your imagination. Every concept, project, and breakthrough you achieve contributes to a larger narrative—a future where technology enhances every facet of human life. From smart cities and personalized healthcare to space exploration and disaster response, the applications of robotics are bound only by our creativity and resolve.

Final Action Points:

- **Reflect:**
  Take time to review and internalize the lessons learned.

- **Plan:**
  Set clear, actionable goals for the next phase of your journey.

- **Collaborate:**
  Engage with communities, share your ideas, and build lasting partnerships.

- **Innovate:**
  Push the boundaries of what's possible, and never be afraid to experiment.

- **Inspire:**
  Your work has the potential to inspire others—lead by example and contribute to the ever-evolving field of robotics.

Rhetorical Question:
Are you ready to turn your vision into reality and be a catalyst for change in the world of robotics? The future is in

your hands, and every step you take brings us closer to a world where technology and humanity thrive together.

Happy innovating, and here's to a future where your contributions shape the next era of robotics!

www.ingramcontent.com/pod-product-compliance
Lightning Source LLC
Chambersburg PA
CBHW080547060326

40689CB00021B/4777